To my wife, Nancy
and to our children
Patrick, Timothy, Jennifer, and Elizabeth

Contents

Love your enemies: do good to them that hate you: and pray for them who persecute and insult you.

Matthew 5:44

Jesus Christ, whom Clotilde asserts to be the Son of the living God, who art said to bestow victory on those who hope in thee, if thou wilt grant me victory over these mine enemies, I will believe in thee and be baptised in thy name.

Clovis, *History of the Franks*

War is the supreme expression of the national will to live and therefore politics must serve war-making.

Eric von Ludendorff, *Der Totale Krieg*

Preface

Some years ago I was researching the theory of "just war" as it was developed by Christian writers in the Middle Ages. I soon discovered that a central theme in this theory, as well as in later international law treatises, was the notion of the "innocent" noncombatant. I realized to my amazement that, crucial as this theme was and is to the vast past and present literature on warfare, no single work was devoted to the subject. To my knowledge, there is still no such study in any language. I decided to try to rectify this monumental oversight of intellectual history. Had I known the extent of the relevant literature, I perhaps would have prudently avoided the prodigious task. Fortunately or not, prudence is not one of my virtues.

My design in this book is two-fold: to induce scholars to pursue this subject in greater depth, and to encourage the intelligent layman to reconsider his options in the face of modern warfare.

I have touched on many subjects in this work. Anthropologists, sociologists, historians, philosophers, lawyers, and soldiers may find cause to complain about what is contained here. However, if all readers recognize themselves as civilians and see this as their history, my presumption will not be in vain.

Richard Shelly Hartigan

Acknowledgments

Many persons contributed to the growth of this book. Some of them deserve a special note of gratitude. My friends and former teachers, Professor William V. O'Brien of Georgetown University and Dom Wulstan Mork, O.S.B., of Marmion Abbey; my colleagues and friends at Loyola University of Chicago, Professors James Wiser and George Szemler, and Professor J. William Hunt at the University of Notre Dame, helped me in various ways. Wanda Welch typed the final manuscript. I am also grateful to the Earhart Foundation for its support, which provided me with much needed time to complete the project. I also acknowledge my debt to my parents, Madge and Joe Hartigan, who reared me in an atmosphere of gentle cynicism, wit and love.

Finally, I thank my wife, Nancy, borrowing the words of John Kenneth Galbraith in *The Age of Uncertainty:*

> I've always been suspicious of authors who use these acknowledgments to proclaim their love for their wives. Most likely it is a cover for secret distaste, occasional beatings, and adulterous yearnings, fulfilled or unfulfilled. But there are exceptions to the best rules.

He then proceeds in his case to do what I must in mine— acknowledge with profound gratitude the patience, support, and critical acumen of my wife.

I

The Forgotten Victim: An Introduction

> To introduce into the philosophy of war a principle of moderation would be an absurdity. War is an act of violence pushed to its utmost bounds.
>
> Carl von Clausewitz, *On War*

The civilian has been pronounced dead. His death knell, which was yet only faintly audible in 1940, sounded loudly for all at 8:15 A.M. on August 5, 1945, in Hiroshima, Japan. Since that date, his obituary has been formally recorded in numerous authoritative sources. Yet in some quarters a nagging doubt remains that the victim may have been buried prematurely.

Is the idea of the civilian an anachronism? Have nuclear weapons and guerrilla warfare forever obliterated the distinction between combatant and noncombatant? In what should be called our Age of Animosity the correct answer would seem to be a reluctant but nonetheless affirmative. Blitzkriegs and obliteration bombings, extermination camps and death by fire storm in Hamburg and Dresden, Hiroshima and Nagasaki—these were the lessons that instructed the survivors of World War II that warfare was now total, not only in the mobilization of resources and resolve but in the annihilation wrought on the innocent and guilty alike. It was always understood that "enemy" was a collective noun but now, through these ordeals, he became an abstraction. Hundreds of thousands of lives were destroyed remotely and anonymously.

Today's college students know of World War II only as history. Yet they share in common with their elders an experience that is the heritage of World War II, that of living in and not yet through the Cold War, SALT treaties notwithstanding. All mankind now shares an expanded vocabulary that includes such

1

words as "nuclear deterrence," "fallout," "massive retaliation," "infiltration" and "guerrilla war."[1]

World War II probably marks a point of no return; it is unlikely that the present superpowers will directly confront each other in conventional warfare. Instead, should such a conflict come upon the world a third time, it is likely to be nuclear, which, we are told, will be quick, clean, almost surgical—and almost surely final. But while waiting for Armageddon and hoping that it will not arrive, the nations have been able to keep their war muscles flexed and in tone through conventional wars, civil wars and recurrent guerrilla wars. In all these conflicts civilian populations have been ruthlessly slaughtered. It is no small irony that the victorious settlement of World War II produced a political climate in which future conflict was bound to flourish, while at the same time it christened a superweapon whose progeny would be weapons systems so awesome that their use can hardly be contemplated for any rational political purpose. There is no irony at all, however, in the fact that the calloused, indifferent and even cynical destruction and depredation visited upon civilian populations (though not then in equal measure) by all parties in World War II is reflected in the contemporary attitude of most people toward the civilian.

This attitude may be fairly and simply characterized as grudging acceptance that there are some innocent noncombatants, combined with a near total fatalism based on the assumption that in present or future wars the civilian cannot be practically isolated or protected. What began with blitzkriegs and progressed through firebombings has culminated in a sad acceptance that all of us are, after all, hostages to potential annihilation by nuclear missiles, or passive spectators of cruel guerrilla warfare in which distinctions between combatant and noncombatant often cannot be made.

What will be presented here is both a mood and an idea. The mood should be obvious, while the idea may require more attention. The status of the civilian today is that of a calculated casualty, to die immediately or after agonizing suffering. The civilian is also a hostage in the political power struggle, since his continued safety depends upon the decision or even caprice of his leaders. This is true if he is a citizen of a major power, which possibly will not take that ultimate step of unleashing the nuclear dogs of war. It is just as true, however, if he lives elsewhere as rice grower, merchant, herdsman, in unstable social and political environments. Here the probability is high that his life will be threatened and endangered, even if he attempts to remain "apolitical" and "uninvolved." It can be asserted as fact that there is little if any conscious, formal concern today about who is a noncombatant, and what should be done about him.

This attitude is the result of a rejection of certain values in the face of modern weapons technology. No value is absolute and only those values are sacred to whom they are.[2] Nevertheless, cultures create values and maintain them tenaciously. One value or principle that has been elaborated and subscribed to by the Western tradition is the belief that certain persons who are clearly not responsible for the prosecution or support of a war ought not to be intentionally attacked or killed. If World War II has been singled out as the conflict most responsible for the demise of noncombatant immunity in the strategic and tactical practice of warfare, it is not in ignorance of war's history. A cursory reading of our species' history verifies that man has been at war almost continuously, probably even before he became Homo sapiens, and that he has been no great respecter of age, sex, or infirmity when confronting his enemy. Yet mankind had made some progress until the twentieth century, a progress rudely halted by World War II.

The validity of this assertion, of course, depends in large part on the definition of progress. Acceptance of biological evolution requires the conclusion that man, while markedly different from other species, is nevertheless still an animal. Man is unique; he can reflect upon his needs and project future solutions. He not only has a history but knows what that history is, and possesses the capacity to forestall its repetition. This makes man a superior being, but an animal nonetheless, an animal that must interact with members of his own and other species, as well as with an often hostile environment. How he interacts is the measure of his progress. A species that manipulates its environment in the light of its felt or reasoned needs and desires not only survives but prospers. Man has been biologically very successful.

There is a third possibility. A species that can no longer cope with its environment will neither progress nor survive, but is doomed to go the way of the dinosaur. If this pattern is true among the lower animal species, why should it be less valid for man? Is it so preposterous to assume that a steady, consistent progress, evidenced by man's capacity to shape to his desire, century after century, the goods and beings of his habitat, has reached a critical point? May not man be flirting with that third alternative that a danger inherent in his technology may fatally destroy his teleology? An affirmative response seems valid since the nations of the world appear to have wilfully rejected a principle that, though often honored only in the breach, has nevertheless marked man as progressive, an enduring species rather than a dying one.

The thesis offered here is transparent. It contends that the lengthy historical immunization of civilians was a step toward survival of the species, and the rejection of this principle by "civilized" peoples in fact and theory in the last three decades is a retrogression that endangers the species. Despite some partial statements, the abandonment of the distinction between the responsible and the nonresponsible in human conflict has not yet been noted as the important phenomenon that it is for species survival. Much has been written about the universal devastation that the human race would suffer if a nuclear holocaust were to occur. Almost as much sage comment has been offered on man's inhumanity to man in guerrilla conflicts. In both categories of potential or actual conflict, however, the conclusion is that it "must not happen," or "it can be no other way." Both conclusions are unsatisfactory and unworthy because they shirk man's responsibility to confront and overcome not only his natural environment but also the environment he himself has created. Had he completely failed this obligation, man would not have progressed because he would not have survived. What must be grasped and accepted now is the fact that mankind is in grave danger of extinction, mutation, or a return to barbarism, but at the same time he also possesses the capacity to prevent such catastrophes. Though it may be true that he has learned little from history, he at least knows that past errors need not be repeated.

The principle of noncombatant or civilian immunity is a theory made concrete in law and practice. It demonstrates how mankind, seemingly driven to lethal intraspecies aggression, had come to control that aggression's worst impact, the intentional slaughter of persons not directly involved in fighting. Now, after nearly eighteen centuries of forging, this societal tool seems shattered and abandoned, the plowshare beaten back into a sword.

The excuse given for this reversal is that modern weapons cannot be used selectively; therefore, civilians can no longer be protected. The error in this rationale is obvious: Weapons do not make choices; men do. Weapons do not decide who their targets shall be, nor how and when they will be used. Man controls the use of weapons, not vice versa. Therefore it is man's decision, his choice whom he shall kill. And it is increasingly apparent that a choice to use weapons of indiscriminate destruction has been made. Mankind may yet follow the dinosaur.

The foregoing may seem an exaggeration. Have the countries of the world really abandoned the notion of the sanctity of innocent human life in theory and in practice? And if they have, would it constitute a fatal rejection, possibly dooming the species? After all, civilians have always been killed without permanent detriment (to the survivors); besides, it may be argued there is an overpopulation problem that could be remedied by another major war. Of course, the remnant population would suffer permanent genetic damage and possess little or no material resources with which to rebuild human society.

This is the era of the United Nations, in which sit representatives of most of the world's political communities. In 1949 the U.N. solemnly announced its Declaration of Human Rights, which was intended to specify and make concrete the members' commitment to humane and civilized existence. That same year the Geneva Convention Relative to the Protection of Civilian Persons in Time of War updated and clarified the traditional immunities guaranteed to civilians. Yet the policies and practices of states before and after the U.N. and Geneva commitments have belied adherence to these principles. It has been argued that if lip service still is being paid to innocent immunity, even when the exigencies or "necessities of war" have required their violation, then at least this represents no formal, theoretical abandonment of the principle. The evidence is otherwise. From "massive retaliation" to "counterinsurgency," military and political planners have written off the civilian.

American military policy in Viet Nam acknowledged the immunity of the civilian population, attack on which would violate the rules of war. But field commanders ignored this stated policy on grounds that strict adherence to it would jeopardize their mission. Since destruction of the enemy was the end of the mission, and the enemy was often impossible to distinguish from the innocent civilian, the only course was to "waste the village." Thus the reasoning ran that if there were civilians in the target area, they should not have been there in the first place, but if they were, it was their misfortune.

The question of battlefield practices in Viet Nam will be dealt with later. Here it is important to note that the soldier in the field was forced to make decisions that should have been made for him by his superiors, not only military but political. In a situation such as Viet Nam, the soldier was required to instantaneously decide whether or not his life was in danger. Should he fire in self-defense on the assumption that a harmless-appearing person might be a guerrilla? Consider the position of the combat soldier: He must obey orders, yet he is instructed not to obey "an unlawful order"; he is trained to kill the "enemy," but he is often unsure of who the enemy is; he is trained to react like a killing automaton, yet he may still remain, even under extreme pressure, a sensitive, humane person. Add to this his lack of instruction and direction with regard to proper treatment of civilians under combat conditions (a situation only partially remedied by the U.S. Army after the Calley–My Lai incident), and the plight of the ordinary soldier can be appreciated. He should not have to choose among complex alternatives in a life-death situation. Such choices can and should be made by his superiors beforehand.

The conclusion must be that the burden of responsibility for the protection of civilians rests not solely with the combat soldier but in large measure with those who decide to prosecute a conflict in which a distinction between the enemy and the civilian cannot adequately be made.

Guerrilla warfare and terrorism aside for the moment, can the case be argued that civilians are immune in theory, if not always in practice, in the value consensus of most of the world? It appears not, but even if it were true that the distinction between combatants and noncombatants is universally accepted, of what consequence is it if occasionally shells rake a Biafran village or a Palestinian refugee camp? These are the fortunes of war, the argument runs, and civil wars are particularly brutal. It is obvious that if practice does not coincide with theory, something is wrong; either commitment to the norms is not real or it is not possible. It is true that most nations claim to subscribe to the notion that civilians should not be intentionally slain, and yet civilians have never before been so involved in so many conflicts, ranging from Africa, through the Middle East, Asia, and Latin America. That is the practice; then what can be the conclusion? There are here two closely related but distinct controlling views.

The first is that today, military practice does not coincide with the theory nor does it respect the principle of civilian immunity because of the nature of modern war. The second view is that the theory is an ideal and has never been taken seriously. Hence it is erroneous to claim that civilian immunity ever has been or could be a practicable norm. Both views represent an indictment of the theory: in the first instance, it is unrealistic under the present circumstances of warfare; in the second, it is a totally unrealizable goal. Since the theory appears fatally flawed, the conclusion follows that only what is practical and necessary can be the active norm of military policy.

As hardheaded and appealing to common sense as this conclusion seems, closer scrutiny reveals that it in no way invalidates the principle of noncombatant immunity; it merely states a preference for a different standard, which in turn reflects the values of those who establish the standards. That modern weapons systems would obliterate combatant and noncombatant alike is a fact; the real issue is, ought they to be used? If military necessity indicates a need for their use, even though millions of civilians may be killed, and if the choice is made to use them regardless of this result, then obviously a preference for civilian immunity has been rejected in favor of military necessity. This is not a question of a theory or principle representing an unattainable ideal or an impractical constraint. Rather it is a forthright rejection of a norm that, if applied, would limit the weapons to be used against an enemy. Given an attitude that places priority on military necessity, it may be stated that the civilian has lost in his bid for protection; policymakers do not consider his immunity to be of high enough priority to guarantee it if military necessity dictates a course of action that would endanger him. A pause is required here to briefly consider the concept of "military necessity," a phrase much in vogue yet seldom subjected to analysis.

Military necessity is a means concept, distinct from a goal concept. Simply, it states that all necessary means should be used to achieve military victory. It does not imply an inordinate use of force but only sufficient force to defeat the enemy. Prudential judgment governs decisions as to the nature and quantity of force employed. Stated thus, military necessity is easy to understand and appears to be a straightforward guide.

The problem arises when the concept is made concrete: Who decides how much force is necessary, and against whom to obtain victory? Again Viet Nam serves as an example, since many American military spokesmen asserted that the best method in American terms would have been the use of nuclear weapons against both the North Vietnamese and the Viet Cong. This common argument was made by high-ranking Army and Navy officers during the Viet Nam conflict. Their assessment was correct in that the destruction of Viet Nam would have ended that war. It also would have probably precipitated a major power conflict.

Clausewitz, whose stark and brutal comment prefaced this chapter, also observed that

To leave a great military enterprise or the plan for one to a purely military judgment and decision is a distinction which cannot
be allowed, and is even prejudicial; indeed, it is an irrational proceeding to consult professional soldiers on the plan of a war, that
they may give a purely military opinion upon what the cabinet
ought to do . . . .[3]

What this Prussian theoretician of war was stating in the nineteenth century is as valid today as it has always been, for war
is not an end in itself but rather a means, and as such should
be subordinate to the end of a restored stable order. As a means,
war is related to larger political goals that are of first priority
for the political leadership and the community.

If politics is truly the peaceful resolution of potential or actual
conflict, then military necessity can be understood as a minor
means subsumed under the more important goal of achieving
peace and stability so that life may continue. War has always
been justified by its participants, but as a means to attain a desired
political end, whether that end was defense, conquest, or per-
suasion of the ideologically unconvinced. War as such is the
absence of politics, since it admits that compromise and toleration of divergent views is no longer possible. But war still remains
the handmaiden of politics in that it is an instrument that can
be used to restore an interrupted political order. Even Hitler at
first related total war to a political end.

What then of military necessity? It is patently obvious that
military necessity has been elevated to an end in itself. How else
can one explain the "scenarios" of defense analysts who describe
the way in which millions will die if the superpowers resort to
nuclear warfare, while they ignore the condition of the human
race in the aftermath? It seems that war has no longer a political
role to play but rather that Ares has replaced Athena, and that
man is committed to his own destruction. What other conclusion is possible when the United States and the U.S.S.R. pride
themselves in the weapons systems they possess and in their
weapons' overkill capability? One can only ask to what political
purpose—that is, to what human purpose?

If, for the sake of argument, recent practice toward the civilian is regarded as an unfortunate lapse and not really indicative—if, in other words, the majority of civilized mankind still reveres the principle of the innocent civilian but can conceive of no way to protect him—then what? The inescapable conclusion must be that man has not solved the problem of his masterful and mastering technology. He has permitted other goals, largely but not wholly ideological, to take precedence in his value orientations. He has abdicated concern to distinguish a combatant from a noncombatant.

No one denies that such a distinction may be extremely difficult. But this begs the question, because it places the burden of distinction on the shoulders of those who would maintain the distinction, when it ought to be on those who claim to adhere to the principle but do not. In short, is innocent immunity a value held by modern political communities? If it is, it is held as one among many values, all striving for place. If it is held today, its position in the heirarchy of political priorities is not very high. If this were not so, then policy and practice would be differently contrived and executed.

Aristotle defined man as a political animal. Others have defined man as an aggressive animal. Both definitions are correct. Homo sapiens often and with relish has killed members of his own species, yet he has also usually evidenced compassion for and tolerance of his fellowman. In the past this ambivertance, this Jekyll-Hyde nature, has been offsetting: life and love have preceded and succeeded death and destruction.

Now it is possible that a point in man's history as a species has been reached where he can no longer afford an insouciant self-indulgence of his nature. He is in mortal peril from his own contrivances. His survival and progress are matters of his control and choice. A reaffirmation of the principle of civilian immunity as his highest priority would represent a major step in guaranteeing his survival and progress.

The following chapters will attempt to fill the gaps in our knowledge of the origins of civilian immunity, so that a full evaluation of the principle's continued worth may be made. The intent is to review the concept of noncombatant, civilian immunity, how it arose from need and intuition and developed into practice and law. The review focuses on the development of this concept in the Western tradition, not because civilian immunity was absent in Asia or Africa but because its present formulation owes its origin and elaboration to European custom, practice, and thought. Despite this element of historical parochialism, what will be revealed is a principle of universal application.

Part I
Theoretical Foundations

II   The Innocent in Primitive and Ancient Warfare

I cut off their heads; I burned them with fire . . . men I impaled on stakes; the city I destroyed . . . the young men and maidens . . . I burned.

Assyrian King Ashurnasirpal II

The evidence is clear and compelling. War is a distinctively human activity, one that man has pursued with zest and imagination since prehistoric times. This is not to overlook the fact that other animals occasionally kill members of their own species. Indeed, violence in nonhuman animal species is common, but purposeful killing within species is not. There is an important difference between the violence visited by one human group on another and the aggression displayed by other animals toward members of their own species. Animal violence is not pursued with the intent of destroying a preidentified "enemy." It is true, of course, that in the struggle to obtain supremacy within, for example, a baboon pack, the fight may end in the death of the weaker party. But most often, the issue is resolved by the flight or submission of the weaker. Antagonism toward another group is much more intense and most of the members of the contesting groups may be ferociously involved. But though the issues are vital for survival (the defense or acquisition of water, food, or territory), the conflict normally ends well short of the participants' death, and never reaches the extreme of the stronger groups' destruction of its "enemy." In short, man's animal brethren do not wage war upon each other. They also do not regularly kill each others' females and young. Such policy is reserved to man.[1]

The reason for man's uniqueness in this respect has yet to be identified, though theories abound.[2] What does appear certain is that man's intraspecies (or intraspecific) violence is due in some measure to his animal origins, his inescapable link with his phylogenetic past. Not surprisingly, men fight each other for the same reasons that other animals fight: to defend or acquire territory and goods. Unlike other species, however, mankind has also fought for the "fun of it," and for what are now called "ideological" reasons. Such motivations are well beyond the capacity of other species.

Though the concern of this study is to trace the historic origins and development of civilian, noncombatant immunity, it is necessary first to enquire what the attitudes and practices toward nonwarriors were in prehistoric societies. This may seem a highly speculative enterprise since, by definition, prehistoric societies left no written records. Offsetting a lack of historical evidence, however, is an abundance of anthropological data detailing the institutions and behavior of primitive peoples. It is highly probable that the warfare practices of modern primitive societies reflect accurately the behavior of prehistoric societies.

The anthropological literature reveals enormous variation in the customs and institutions of primitive peoples.[3] This is to be expected. But it also shows a remarkable number of constants, especially in the conduct of war. Several of these stand out.

First, it appears that prehistoric man shared with his historic successors a dual moral code, one of which applied to members of his group and might be called "internal," the other applying to everyone else outside the group, an "external" code. The internal code prescribed and proscribed behavior that would guarantee the survival of the group. No stealing, no murder, reverence for the old and the dead, were rules that, if followed, would produce a stable and cooperative band. The external code, on the other hand, often sanctioned behavior forbidden within the group. Stealing, killing, and lying to strangers were considered laudable, because basically, "stranger" meant "enemy," a competitor for the necessities of survival.[4]

A second characteristic of primitive man's attitude toward intergroup violence was that such violence was the business of the male.⁵ "First and foremost among the services which the savage man performs is that of defending his group and fighting its battles. . . . War among less-civilized peoples is not the business of a selected few; it is the occupation of every adult male."⁶ Women and children suffered as a result of their group's conflict, but they themselves were not active participants.

Given the prevailing and pervasive primitive attitudes of fear and hatred of the enemy and male monopoly on fighting, a final general characteristic of primitive warfare followed predictably: the most vulnerable among the enemy would suffer the most. In a pattern of warfare devoid of laws or regulations, among societies whose tribal mores reduced women to the status of property, it is hardly surprising that they and their young would be the objects of the greatest cruelty. The savage mind could be pictured as logically concluding that the most economic use of his energies in war would be to guarantee that he would not have to face his enemy again. One way to achieve this result was to eliminate the source of future supply.

Gradually and unevenly, some human societies escaped from the precariousness of their ancestors' existence. More predictable food supplies and greater ingenuity in providing shelter and defense permitted these societies to make the leap from savagery to civilization. Historic man was born. The city became both a tool by which he forged a more secure existence, and a target to those of his still primitive fellowmen who had not yet learned his lessons. Settled agricultural living was now possible, and with it, the firm establishment of an institution that, ironically enough, would serve to mitigate the worst cruelty of primitive warfare. Women and children were no longer summarily slain; instead, they were now enslaved.

In the twentieth century, when human slavery is almost universally condemned, it is difficult to imagine that in the not too distant past it " 'marked a decided improvement in human manners.' It was, in truth, a great humanitarian advance."⁷ Though the term "humanitarian" credits an unworthy degree of rational sensitivity to man, the slave-maker, it is true that he became aware of the economic advantage to be gained from enslaving a con-

quered enemy. It is also true that, in most instances, bondage
was preferable to death.

Ancient historic warfare, therefore, presents an altered picture
from its prehistoric predecessor in some respects, though in other
respects there remained a great continuity with the past. For warriors only recently removed from barbarism, relapses to the old
ways could be expected. The heroic literature of Western culture
is replete with slaughters of the innocent. But often such lapses
were condemned by the chroniclers, the tragic Chorus, or the
gods. What seemed to be dawning was an awareness that the
vulnerable, the defenseless, ought not to be the mortal victims
of war.

The Greek, Roman, and Hebrew philosophers, poets, and
prophets provide ample texts decrying the slaughter of prisoners,
women, and children. That it was necessary for them to condemn these practices obviously indicates that such behavior was
still widespread. Thus, Euripides in *The Trojan Women* tells of
Andromache's heartbreak over the imminent murder of her son
by the conquering Greeks, and her judgment of them as barbarians,[8] while Sallust ascribed Rome's decline to its brutality in
dealing with Carthage.[9]

As typical as such violence against the nonwarrior must
have been in ancient civilizations, also typical was criticism
of it by the ancient authors. One student of these classical
authors was Hugo Grotius, the father of modern international law. In his *On the Law of War and Peace*, Grotius
provides a virtual encyclopedia of classical references on the
necessity to respect age, sex, and occupation during warfare.
From the Old Testament to the Roman writers of the
Christian era, he cites exhortations to be merciful to those
among the enemy who are innocent. One representative opinion
is Polybius, who wrote,

> It becomes good men not to wage a war of annihilation even with
> the wicked, but to proceed only so far that crimes may be remedied
> and corrected; and not to involve the innocent in the same punish-
> ment as the guilty, but even to spare those who are guilty for the
> sake of the innocent.[10]

The cultural refinements and technological progress of the great ancient civilizations is well known. What is also known is the constancy of warfare among these civilizations, and between them and their less advanced neighbors. But what is curious about ancient warfare is the marked difference between theory and practice in the manner of conduct toward the innocent. While merciful treatment of the defenseless was preached as an ideal, and condemned when not accorded in fact, the nonwarrior was no more immune from attack than his or her prehistoric predecessor. Even less secure were captured soldiers who were usually put to the sword. A peace movement such as the Olympic Games was in reality nothing more than a periodic armistice, while Plato's urging of mercy for a conquered enemy applied only to fellow Greeks and was essentially pragmatic in that mercy would be rewarded in kind if at some future date today's winners might become tomorrow's losers.[11] Finally, institutionalized slavery in ancient times, though sparing many who otherwise would have been put to death, can hardly be seen as anything more than exploitation for economic gain.

Thus, the practice of the ancient world in the treatment of the nonwarrior population had barely advanced from precivilizational behavior. Indeed, it may be argued that with civilization and the greater group homogeneity it produced, there occurred a hardening of attitude toward the enemy, sometimes a deeper ideological fervor, and an increased reluctance to show mercy.

If this is true, how can the words of Polybius and so many other ancient authors be explained? Was theirs a special vision in their time? Probably so, since the ancient warrior, if literate at all, was no philosopher, nor was his king.

One reason that ancient men of letters were repelled by indiscriminate slaughter can be found in the very milieu that allowed them to become men of letters in the first place, the city. The Greek *polis* and the *urbs* of the Romans were the cultural wombs within which the *civis*, or citizen, could live secure from daily fear, fight, and flight, a stability and predictability of existence that provided time for reflection, and with that reflection came arts, letters, and sciences. The city, urban living, with shelter secure from the elements and food supplies assured, meant civilization. It was the *sine qua non* of civilization.

However, ancient man was forced to pay a price for the luxury of that reflection afforded him by urban living. He had to organize and institutionalize a portion of the city's population for its defense. Thus was born the soldier, and his alter ego, the civilian.[12]

The poets, philosophers, and priests of Sumer, Egypt, Persia, and Greece were civilians. They shared with the merchant, the mother, and the child a vested interest in a life uninterrupted by strife. Little wonder that they decried the indiscriminate killing of their kind.

The sages did not produce a rationale or general theory that justified sparing the nonsoldier. If warfare among peoples had occurred since time immemorial, and if its practice had always included cruelty against the defenseless, why now should these be spared? Intuition indicated that they should be; custom decreed otherwise. Perhaps the reason for this lacuna was the fact that no notion of "humanity" had yet evolved in the mind of Western man. He was still a citizen of a particular city or kingdom, his vision bounded by its territory, and his concern present and parochial. The ancient world required the notion of *homonoia*.

Aristotle had spoken the last word on the worth of the *polis*, the city-community, when he declared that a person who resided outside the *polis* was either a beast or a god, subhuman or superhuman—but not human.[13] He also summarized his attitude toward non-Greeks in his advice to his protégé, Alexander, that all non-Greeks were barbarians and should be treated as such.[14]

Alexander the Great, however, ignored his mentor's teaching and sought to supplement his conquests with a union of peoples—not to destroy the Persian Empire but to subsume it and thereby mix the fruits of Greek and Middle Eastern culture and power. The best example of this was his marriage of 10,000 of his Macedonian troops to Persian women in Susa in 324 B.C., a year before his death.[15]

Shortly after, the philosophy of Stoicism was founded in Athens by Zeno of Citium. Among its tenets was a simple truth: All men are brothers, since they share reason and thus a common humanity. The notion of *homonoia,* "brotherhood," as a theoretical concept was introduced to Western thought. When coupled with Alexander's practical intuition and policies, Hellenism was born, and with it both a theoretical and practical basis for noncombatant immunity.

The spread of Greek culture throughout the ancient world, Hellenism, had a revolutionary impact, for at its heart was a transpolitical message: The *polis* as a self-contained, all-sufficing community was dead. In its place there arose a sense of commonality among men of different cultures and a conviction that the traditional parochial loyalties to city or kingdom were obsolete. Alexander's conquests and the later Greek philosophies, most notably Stoicism, initiated and supported these innovations. The Roman Empire and Christianity were logical continuations, historically, of dynastic and intellectual forces set in motion centuries before them.

Hence, from the near-total barbarism of prehistoric conflict, Western man to the pre-Christian era had developed a certain sense or feeling that some members of an enemy population ought to be spared. What had not developed was a consistent, coherent theoretical justification for such immunity, nor a precise definition of who should be considered immune, nor the practical apparatus to provide such immunity. The foundations, however, were established, and with the marriage of Roman order and Christian theory a unified structure would be erected. The civilian was not yet fully defined, much less protected—this was still a centuries-long task—but at least a beginning had been made in regard to the morality of intergroup homicide. Western man was on the verge of distinguishing between the guilty and the innocent in war.

III

"Innocence" in Early Christian Thought

> Peace should be the object of your desire. War should be waged only as a necessity and waged only that through it God may deliver men from that necessity and preserve them in peace.
>
> Augustine, *Letter to Boniface*

May a Christian ever justifiably kill his fellow man? Can he serve in the military profession, knowing that he may contribute directly or indirectly to the death of an enemy? Is a war ever just? For almost fifteen hundred years a majority of Christians have answered these questions affirmatively. They have done so with the confidence that there is no inherent contradiction between the awful necessities of having to kill and the exhortations to peace and love expressed by Jesus in the New Testament. With periodic exceptions, the dominant Christian tradition has rejected pacifism in favor of a limited accceptance of the necessity to sometimes slay an enemy and defend a homeland. The formalized principles that support this view are popularly referred to as the Christian theory of just war.

Although not formal articles of faith, the corpus of principles and interpretations known as just war theory have constituted an authoritative moral reference since its basis was established by St. Augustine, Bishop of Hippo, in the late fourth and early fifth centuries. Through the Church it pervaded the moral consciousness of Western culture. As the Church's power waxed, so too did the authority of its social ethic, which became for centuries the unchallenged normative standard of European culture. Moreover, its influence has been felt far beyond the Christian community. In the process of elaboration it encompassed far more than Augustine originally intended, and in its final form it provided a philosophic cornerstone for the positive international law of war. This theoretical legacy of the Christian medieval Church is impressively subtle, comprehensive, and, above all, confident.

But the mind of the Church was not always so set, especially on the subjects of intentional killing and the justice of war. It is a measure of Augustine's greatness that he was able to synthesize a number of divergent theological and philosophical positions at a crucial point in European history. The beginning of the notion of "social innocence" in Western thought is revealed in the laborious and ingenious effort of Augustine to produce a Christian compromise with conflict—in other words, to make peace with war.

Augustine's views on war and killing, and the polemical stance into which he was forced, reflect the attitudes he inherited from earlier writers and the impact of contemporary circumstances. He began writing his major work, *City of God,* in 413 A.D., three years after Alaric and his Goths took possession of Rome. Though Christianity had triumphantly survived the persecutions of previous centuries, many non-Christian Romans still regarded it with suspicion or hatred. Not surprisingly, they blamed the Christians for the Empire's collapse, villifying them as unpatriotic citizens. For thirteen years, Augustine occupied himself with rebutting these charges in his famous apologia.

There is another and perhaps more significant respect in which Augustine was a polemicist. While his intention was to refute the pagan critics of Christianity, in order to achieve this end he also had to refute a position taken by many of his fellow Christians. Lurking in the background was the fact that some of the Church's most prestigious authorities had embraced pacifism, a fact that lent credibility to the pagan charge that Christians, if they refused to serve the Empire as soldiers, were disloyal. Augustine was therefore in the position of a man facing his enemy without being certain of support from his allies in the rear.

Was the Christian, bound as he was to the law of love, ever permitted to wilfully take another human life? Since the Gospels seemed to extol a life of peace and forbearance, many early Christians concluded that withdrawal from public life, and especially avoidance of military service, was required by Jesus of his followers. Writers such as Tertullian, Origen, and Lactantius were the most intransigent, while pacifist leanings can also be perceived in the works of Minucius Felix, Justin Martyr, Clement of Alexandria, Cyprian, Irenaeus, and Athenagoras. This was a formidable array of revered patriarchs and intellectuals. Their views of Jesus' message and the Christian's salvation could not be lightly dismissed.

Jesus' intent, as it survives in the New Testament texts, is ambiguous. He reproves Peter for drawing his sword (Matthew 26:52); but he also praises the Roman Centurion for his faith (Matthew 8:5–13), offering no condemnation of his profession. Jesus enjoins his audience to mercy, as his Father is merciful (Luke 6:36). In Paul's Epistle to the Romans (12:19) there is a clear warning against taking vengeance in this life, a recourse that was reserved to the Lord. However, as Luke reports, one who has no purse ought to sell his cloak and purchase a sword (Luke 22:36). Most famous is the encounter between Jesus and the Herodians and Pharisees, in which arises the question of paying tribute to Caesar. Jesus instructs, "Render to Caesar the things that are Caesar's; and to God the things that are God's" (Mark 12:17). Thus there was ample room for confusion about Jesus' attitude toward violence, killing, and obedience to the public authority.

There was no doubt, however, in the mind of Tertullian. Apparently he was a pacifist before and after he joined a radically eschatological sect, the Montanists. He asserts unequivocally that no Christian may serve by the sword, since the Lord disarmed every soldier when He took Peter's sword.[1] In a later work he expresses himself even more sharply, declaring that soldiering cannot possibly be a lawful occupation for Christians since the Lord had declared that he who uses the sword shall perish by it.[2] Quotations can be multiplied to demonstrate the pacifism of Origen and Lactantius, as well. These writers, however, were acknowledged extremists who, though influential to a degree, did not represent a generally accepted and formalized opinion. In fact, to the extent to which a Christian consensus existed on military service, with its implied confirmation of the ethics of killing a fellow human being, it gave tacit approval.[3]

If isolated writers fulminated about Christian participation in war, most Church officials and theologians appear to have followed a policy of "watchful waiting," as Adolf Harnack termed it.[4] The Cyprians and Clements, though they did enjoin against the immorality of soldiering, seem most concerned about the temptations of camp life and the vices of soldiers. There is nothing in their writings to indicate that they were thoroughgoing pacifists. We also have the evidence of the Church Councils, which at this time were very powerful. There is not a single known conciliar decree against military service prior to the time of Constantine. When tolerance of Christianity was accorded by Constantine, we find, to the contrary, that at the Council of Arles (314 A.D.) a canon decreed excommunication for anyone who deserted the Imperial armies, even in time of peace.[5] In other words, the Christian Church was not pacifist, either in theory or in practice, though many of its prominent apologists were. Instead, by Augustine's time it could boast a recent but intense support for citizens' military duty. On these grounds the Bishop of Hippo might have convincingly challenged the pagan detractors of his religion. Yet he seems to have been disturbed by the problem of reconciling the required disposition of love with military ferocity. Tertullian may have been outvoted, but he and his fellow pacifists had exposed the rawest of nerves for a sensitive Christian.

Augustine's ideas on most matters are as complex and inconsistent as his life and personality. At one point or another in his career he embraced the philosophy of Neoplatonism, the heresy of Manichaeism, and, by his own admission, uncounted mistresses. In order to trace his attitudes toward killing, one must search through a number of texts besides *City of God,* in which he establishes the justifiability of war. Given the proper circumstances and disposition of will, or motivation, war is seen as a proper means to achieve the good end of a restored moral order. That violence and death are required to achieve this result is lamentable but unavoidable. The Christian may therefore wage a just war.

Interestingly, this conclusion is not anticipated in Augustine's earlier writings; nor is the extremely harsh position he takes toward a public enemy consistent with his stated views on private killing. His extremely influential work on free will,[6] composed long before *City of God,* contained an argument to which he often returned. In this dialogue, Augustine and his friend, Evodius, explore the nature of evil, especially as it relates to the act of murder. Augustine maintains that murder is always evil, regardless of its motivation, and in defining a murderous act he agrees that what the state prohibits as unlawful killing is equally prohibited by the moral law. This legal prohibition, however, is not inclusive enough, for there are situations in which the law permits an individual to kill an unjust aggressor, an assailant, for example, who attempts to rob or injure him; but for Augustine the possible loss of one's life or goods is not sufficient justification to take another's life, this being a greater evil. He does not feel that the law permitting self-protection is unjust, merely that it is inadequate for the Christian.[7]

To permit self-defense, even to the killing of an assailant, is for most people legally and morally justifiable as the choice of a lesser over a greater evil, for "it is far more dreadful that an innocent person should suffer violence than that the assailant should be killed by the intended victim."[8] But for the Christian, upon whom extraordinary demands are made, the law of love requires a literal turning of the other cheek. The Christian ought not to avail himself of his legal right to self-defense but should rather be guided by the divine law of love, which enshrines all human life, even that of an enemy, as inviolate. Augustine later reaffirms this view in a letter to a friend: "In regard to killing men so as not to be killed by them, this view does not please me."[9] His position on private self-defense was unqualifiedly pacifist. For him the life of even an evil aggressor could not be jeopardized by resistance. In short, one must suffer evil rather than participate in it.

One would suppose that Augustine's attitude toward war, with its slaughter of innocent and guilty alike, would be one of equal repugnance. Remarkably, the opposite is true. Instead of a diatribe against public defense and killing, he offers a succinct formula for determining when aggressive warfare may be waged and under what circumstances the man of righteousness may slay the evildoer. The final irony of this seemingly inconsistent moral stance is that by providing an ethical justification for war among nations, Augustine lays the foundation for a normative structure that will eventually proclaim the inviolable innocence of persons among the enemy. If Augustine's moral eyesight was sometimes myopic, or even crossed, he at least perceived the need for some modification of the radical extremes of the ancient world: all wars are not wrong, nor is all warfare permissible. Rather, moral and religious limitations should guide and determine the limits of violence.

But when is war just and when might killing be permitted to the Christian? In every instance wherein he condemns private killing, Augustine adds the qualification that human life may be taken in the name of public authority. When Evodius queries him about the status of a soldier who kills, or a judge or executioner who puts a criminal to death, Augustine replies that these individuals are not murderers.[10] He points out that soldiers are required to kill the enemy; if they do not, they are subject to punishment by the military authorities. Once again in his letter to Publico, where he states flatly that killing does not please him, he adds, "unless perhaps it should be a soldier or a public official. In this case, he does not do it for his own sake, but for others or for the state to which he belongs, having received the power lawfully and in accord with his public character."[11] Simply stated, when a person acts in a public capacity and without motives of passion or vengeance, then, as the lawful agent of the state, he may kill. The reasons for this exception to the divine prohibition against killing are threefold. First, the soldier or official is merely carrying out a function of the public will and is not therefore morally responsible for the death and suffering he inflicts.[12] Secondly, and following from the first conclusion, such an individual acts as an agent of the public justice "or the wisdom of government," to which, thirdly, the objectives of his actions are "wicked men."

Augustine makes clear his basic distinction between the action one takes privately and the activity of the same individual in another, public role.[13] As a citizen, a *civis*, a man may be called upon to defend the community and as such to discharge his obligation to aid in restoring a violated moral order. This distinction exemplifies an oft-noted characteristic of the Augustinian philosophy of history, the difference between the orders of charity and justice. In the Christian's private life, the order of charity or love should be the criterion for behavior. His guide should be the counsels of perfection, and his ideal the life of Jesus. But in this too imperfect world, where "awful necessities" require less than perfect response, the norm must be justice, and policy must be based on obedience to lawful authority. For Augustine temporal peace possesses a moral dimension. Violence to that peace, an unjustified, aggressive war by one state against another, is more than merely a legal *delict;* it constitutes a violation of moral justice. As such it is morally equivalent to a private criminal action against a state. Thus Augustine is not inconsistent in maintaining that certain actions are permitted persons in the public order of justice that are forbidden in the private order of charity, since there are wicked men abroad who would otherwise disrupt the peace. Such miscreants must be punished, even if it means that they must be killed. To do so is not only morally permissible but morally required.

Even though Augustine condoned the taking of human life under official auspices, we cannot conclude that he approved some kind of license to kill while wearing a badge. On the contrary, a soldier was permitted to kill only in a just war, and it is the conditions that make a war just to which we now turn. So important did Augustine's definition of just war become that it is worth quoting at length. "Just wars are usually defined as those which avenge injuries, when the nation or city against which warlike action is to be directed has neglected either to punish wrongs committed by its own citizens or to restore what has been unjustly taken by it."[14] What is involved in this definition is both the notion of moral vengeance—justified wrath and intended punishment against an evildoer—and the recognition of material or objective *delict,* that is, crime. The crime or fault will be determined by what is customary practice among nations; the sacking of a city, refusal to grant passage, failure to redress a grievance, and most instances of self-defense are proper excuses for retaliation.[15] The other, moral dimension, however, is equally significant, because it provides the "just" side with a spiritual reference frame, a kind of transcendental guideline that directs and justifies its actions in terms of a standard of righteousness external to the actors who are actually performing them. It provides, in effect, a rationale for the crusader mentality. This attitude, stemming from an ideologically derived self-confidence in the rightness of one's cause, is a major characteristic of Western conflict justification. It does not have its origins in Augustine's thought, but there can be no doubt that his *auctoritas,* dominant as it was for so many centuries, irrevocably stamped with approval the posture of the just warrior, the Richard *Coeur de Lion* engaged in righteous struggle against an evil foe.

Augustine's conditions for just war may be summarized as follows: There must be a just cause, an actual objective infringement of the legal order; the war must be declared by and carried out under the auspices of the proper legal authority; and its motivation must be to attain peace, which is the only proper end of war. But even though just war is an act of retributive justice, it may not be carried out in a spirit of passion or vengeance.[16] Such an attitude neutralizes the justice of the cause and renders unjust a further prosecution of the conflict. With further refinements this statement remains the essential theoretical position of the major Christian denominations with regard to a justified war or *bellum justum.* The intent, the causes, and the conditions of just war constitute a theory that in contemporary positive international law is referred to as *jus ad bellum* or the justification for war. This can be viewed as the structure, the broad-brush limits that provide, as they did in Augustine's mind, the rationale for inter-state conflict. It is within this structure that an equally important body of conceptual limitations was to arise which is given the title of *jus in bello,* or just action during war, by which is meant a consideration of *debitus modus,* the proper conduct that should guide the contenders.

It was noted earlier that there is a peculiar irony in Augustine's contribution to just war theory. He undoubtedly provided a masterful synthesis of ancient and Christian thought (and to a certain extent practice) on the legal and moral conditions of justified war. Far from being a warmonger, he exhibited a most doleful mood with regard to the necessity to engage in bloodshed even for a rightful cause, and a very strong implication in his work is that few wars can indeed be just, since among other conditions, one must have near perfect knowledge that the enemy is truly morally guilty. Such a condition could rarely be met. Yet an unfortunate lapse is also apparent in Augustine's vision that is less a fault of commission than of omission—the result, we might suspect, of an overtheologizing on the subject. Evidence of this tendency is his consistent emphasis on the wickedness of the enemy, an attitude that is certainly the result of his total view of conflict in moral terms. The weakness of such a stance is obvious—it ascribes a condition of communal guilt and universal evil to the enemy, which, when carried to its logical conclusion, precludes any necessity to act mercifully toward the enemy population.

To be sure, there are passages in his works where he explicitly enjoins against conducting a war in a spirit of vengeance. More practically, he insists that faith must be kept with the enemy and mercy shown to those who can no longer fight or who are captured. Massacres, wanton violence, and profanation of sanctuaries are prohibited, as are attacks on women and children.[17] Though Augustine claims that such merciful conduct distinguishes the Christian at war from the barbarian, the fact is that a primitive form of noncombatant immunity already existed to some extent among the ancients. He is merely restating what was theoretically accepted by some of his civilized predecessors. As it stands, Augustine's views on the proper conduct of war and the immunity of certain persons and places is an eloquent exhortation to limit even justified violence, and his statements should be accorded their due as contributing to a more humane prosecution of public violence. No doubt that was his intention.

To complicate the matter, however, in logic his theory of just war cannot comfortably accommodate the notion of innocents among the enemy who deserve to be protected during the hostilities, that is, while victory may be still in doubt. It was Christian to be merciful toward a beaten foe who could no longer cause harm, but what of one's conduct toward members of the enemy population who meant no harm in the first place? Augustine's failure to address himself to this question is all the more remarkable when his great sensitivity and private ethical pacifism are recalled. It seems as though the requirements to vindicate justice obviate all other considerations, and though he recognizes that the innocent may accidentally suffer in the process, he consigns this to necessity and is perfectly resigned to it. Thus, to a judge who, through ignorance, condemns an innocent man to death, Augustine offers the advice that he not trouble himself but rather pray to God, "from my necessities deliver Thou me."[18] To Boniface, a military man who is faced with many difficult moral choices in the performance of his duty, he suggests that the soldier make his interior peace but by no means abandon his duty.[19]

Two aspects of Augustine's thought provide probable rationales for his position. The first is that while he admits that there may be innocent persons among the enemy population, he does not believe that this will regularly be the case. For Augustine, who believed in an intimate relationship between individual and social morality, it is highly doubtful that an unjust nation will be populated by good or just citizens. Just as Lot's family was an exceptional minority in the city of Sodom, so it seems that Augustine presumes that most often innocent men will be a small minority in the unjust state. In addition, the guilt with which Augustine is concerned is an interior spiritual condition; so too its obverse, innocence, will be an interior disposition, impossible to ascertain or to ascribe with certainty to any particular individuals.

The second basis for Augustine's view is more explicit. It is his frequently expressed attitude that death is merely a physical evil and to suffer this fate is far better than to be guilty of bad motivation or vice. Augustine believed that death was not the evil to be shunned in war. If guiltless people were slain in a just war it was lamentable but not condemnable, for God often permits the innocent to be scourged with the guilty in this life, "though in eternity they quite escape punishment."[20] Those who kill while prosecuting a just war are condemned by Augustine only if they do so from a motive of private passion, or if they continue to slay when it is no longer necessary. This fact is significant because it means that no moral guilt is attached to the slaughter of any particular persons. The innocence or guilt of those attacked is of no consequence in determining the guilt of the attacker; the only factors that constrain him are the subjective ones of his own intent and his estimation of military necessity. Any objective determination as to who are innocent or guilty among the enemy is not only impossible but is also irrelevant.[21]

It would be hardly worth considering this aspect of Augustine's thought in such detail were it not for the fact that his view of just war as a retributive, moral act was to dominate the Christian philosophy of war for almost a thousand years. Even the innovative genius of Thomas Aquinas succumbs to Augustine's theory. It is only when God's presence in the world is no longer so confidently asserted, in the waning of the Middle Ages, that his influence in this matter diminishes.

An overly rigid interpretation of Augustine's moralistic and subjective views on just war by later writers had a retarding effect on the application of the Christian ethic of mercy to war's conduct. But herein lies an irony, for it is doubtful that without his synthetic structuring of war's permissibility within a Christian commonwealth an eventual concern for *debitus modus* would have occurred at all. Rigid and subjective as it was, Augustine's *jus ad bellum* was the necessary theoretical framework within which to speculate about war's proper conduct. Since the first step in problem solving is definition of the problem, Augustine deserves full credit for his insistence that war is not an inevitable phenomenon, incapable of control by the human mind. Instead he perceives in war a purposiveness and, though one may not agree with him as to what the purpose is, he does at least clearly state that war is not an end in itself. As a means to achieve a goal or goals it is inherently limitable. Augustine saw war's purpose as the means to restore a peaceful order, while correctly chastizing those who would disturb that order. As such, war was a public act that should, therefore, by necessity be circumscribed by moral limits. From a later vantage point, his view may appear incomplete and flawed by certain doctrinaire premises. Nevertheless, he is the first major thinker in the Western tradition to see war as a problem susceptible of solution, to define what he felt were its proper dimensions, and to insist that it is not its own justification. What he bequeathed to his successors is not so much a doctrine or a finished theory, but rather, and perhaps more significantly, an optimistic view of man's place in history.

The Christian was, for Augustine, a pilgrim, struggling against temptations to vice and striving to live a life as a citizen of God's City. Though difficult, the task was not impossible. Augustine's belief that there was divine intervention in history, manifested through the presence of Jesus, was the support of his world view. This view held that history was now irrevocably altered so that its *telos* or end was predictable. This fact of Augustine's thought belies the popular image of him as the gloomy and self-critical theologian, overwhelmed by a sense of guilt. In fact, it was the very universalism of Christianity, its salvific meaning for all men, that inspired Augustine's vision of the possibility of a true Christian Commonwealth in which all might participate and all might be ruled by an ordered justice. Intellectually, the time was ripe for such a view. The universal brotherhood of mankind, as preached by the Stoic philosophers of Greece and Rome, provided a theoretical base for the real, practical unity that had been actually achieved by Roman law and the institutions of the Empire itself. For Augustine the notion of Christian personalism, of equality before a Creator, was a logical capstone to these other views. For him the world was actually potentially one—ethically and politically. Here is the measure and implication of his optimism.

Given such a world view, he approached the phenomenon of public conflict with both a more profound and more expanded attitude than his classical predecessors. Wars could be just, but their justice depended on proper motivation as much as conformity to accepted legal norms. The enemy could be slain but only reluctantly, only within limits, and never out of hatred. Perhaps here is the best demonstration of his originality, for he goes well beyond the notions of his great master, St. Ambrose. Ambrose, too, had preached justice, mercy, and forbearance when dealing with an enemy, restating verbatim the injunction of his own pagan authority, Cicero.[22] Augustine, however, raises the customs of warfare to a new plane by infusing the humanistic sympathy of victor for vanquished with the imperative of Divine charity. He did not himself perceive the implications of this innovation nor draw the fullest possible conclusions from it. But the ingenuity of his message was not ignored by nor lost on later writers. It is in this sense, and with this understanding of his work, that we can verify an earlier observation that Augustine provided the structure within which a more sophisticated theory of "social innocence" could be developed.

The modern classification of the civilian, the noncombatant who should be treated in some special, protective fashion, rests on an assumption of nonresponsibility. In ancient times there existed a practice of sorts in which certain classes of the enemy were treated differently from the armed combatants. The prohibitions against killing the unarmed women, children, and aged among the conquered enemy stemmed primarily from the consideration that they posed no threat to the victor. Gradually, what may be called a more legalistic appraisal began to intrude itself in the sense that the fact of nonparticipation in active fighting by certain persons among the enemy was sufficient to disqualify them as legitimate "targets" in war. But this development was excruciatingly slow in coming and neither the ancient nor the early Christian worlds embraced this attitude. Instead, the custom

of war with regard to the civilian centered on the pragmatic determination of "do not unto me and I shall not do unto you" or
"spare my women this time, and when the wheel turns, I will
spare yours." Besides, women and children were far more useful
commodities alive—a dead slave was useless.

The writings of the most influential early Christian authorities
reveal a satisfaction or agreement with the long-standing custom
of the ancient world. Only with Augustine do we discern a groping
and hesitant articulation of a guilt-innocence opposition that is
not dependent upon the usual separation of women and inferiors
from the soldiery. In other words, what Christian thought was
developing was an ethical rationale or justification for mercy that
would go beyond the dictates of military necessity and pragmatic
economics. This is the basis Augustine provided. With Augustine
the early Church shed its ambivalence with regard to the public
duty to kill. The rule for the fifth century Christian soldier was
the same as that for his pagan ancestor—no unnecessary slaughter.
But a new dimension had been added: no slaughter at all with
desire for glory or revenge. This may seem a too subtle distinction, of little practical worth. On the contrary, its effect on the
humanization of warfare was to prove as great as the invention
of the stirrup in the technology of medieval warfare.

IV

"Just War" in the Middle Ages

It is customary to term just those wars which have the aim of avenging injuries . . . .

Gratian, *Decretum*

Therefore, it is in no way lawful to slay the innocent.

Thomas Aquinas, *Summa theologica*

The intellectual history of the Middle Ages is so dominated by the authority of Sts. Augustine and Thomas Aquinas that one tends to dismiss as marginal the work of the scholars who labored during the almost nine centuries that elapsed between the times of the two giants. It is true that from the death of Augustine until the rediscovery of Aristotle in the West in the thirteenth century, which served as the catalyst for Aquinas' work, there were no comparable intellects. Yet one cannot ignore the contributions of the philosophers, theologians, and lawyers of this period. Originality was not characteristic of them but attention to detail was. Their work is a bridge over the chasm of the dark period in European history, when an empire succumbed to its own weaknesses and spawned with its demise a crisis of political disorder unique in Western civilization. An examination of this nearly nine-century period creates the impression that the intellect of Europe was dormant, trying little new, perhaps only consolidating its gains. No creative bursts appeared until the remarkable synthesis of Aquinas; but his synthesis would have been impossible without the dogged efforts of his predecessors.

A chief figure in this era was St. Isidore (560–636), the archbishop of Seville. He was a towering figure in his generation, both in and beyond his native Spain.[1] His thoughts and writings linked the classical past with the Greco-Roman-Spanish culture of his origin and, most important, his knowledge of Roman law enabled him to blend a practical expertise with his philosophical insight.

His most significant work was the *Originum seu etymologiarum libri XX,* the *Etymologies.*[2] It was not an original work; its value lay in its encyclopedic compilation of past masters' writings. On justifiable war, however, Isidore does introduce a new factor, a juridical notion derived from the old Roman law requiring that war must be properly declared before hostilities may commence.[3]

In other respects he follows the criteria laid down by Augustine: The object of war must be to repulse an invading enemy, avenge a wrong, and punish those guilty of breaching the peace; but he adds that war may be just if its aim is to recover stolen goods (*de rebus repetitis*). After Augustine's pronouncements on just war, it was generally accepted that defensive war was just by definition. Isidore provides for the first time a potential theoretical justification for offensive wars. His elaboration of the Augustinian theme was to have crucial consequences for the future of just war theory.[4]

Other important successors of Augustine include Ives of Chartres (1040–1116?). His comments are contained in the discussions of homicide in Book VIII of his *Panormia* and Part X of his *Decretum.* Though he adds nothing original to the formalized theory of just war, his reliance on Augustine and Isidore for his definitions is revealing. On the legitimacy of self-defense, the justice of a war to defend one's community, the moral innocence of soldiers who kill in battle, the justice of wars waged by the Israelites, and the legitimacy of the military profession, Ives quotes Augustine.[5] On the conditions under which a war may be initiated justly, he quotes Isidore. Ives, who was considered by his contemporaries an authority in his own right, exemplifies the degree to which a then-developed "Augustinian position" on just war held sway.

All that was needed to ratify this opinion in a final form was forthcoming in the writings of Gratian, who published in 1150 a widely circulated compilation of "decretals." This laborious editing of Church rules or canons was to form the first part of the *Corpus juris canonici,* or code of canon law, the body of legal dicta that constituted the rules governing the internal structure of the Catholic Church. With only insignificant changes,

Gratian subscribes to the Augustinian formulation of the conditions justifying offensive warlike action.[6]

It has been correctly pointed out that the *Decretum* of Gratian is a decisive formulation in the development of just war theorizing.[7] The *Decretum* ended a period in which the teachings of Augustine on war had been pruned and reduced to a few essential ideas and statements, which hardened into a foundation of thought universally accepted as basic. Augustine's teachings on war and killing had become the common heritage of medieval writers. The stage was set for a period of systematic development and elaboration of these accepted principles.

Two schools of writers contributed to this development, each working within a slightly different framework. One group, the canonists, carried forward the work of Gratian to define in precise legal terms the concrete circumstances under which war could be justified. The other group, the speculative theologians, were concerned chiefly with the elaboration of essential moral and philosophical principles. It is dangerous, of course, to distinguish too sharply between these writers, whose premises and conclusions were often identical. The canonists were just as concerned as the theologians about the moral problems involved in war; they simply reached their conclusions by a different route. Both schools assumed as valid starting points the teachings of Augustine, and both ended very often with the same conclusions. Yet there was a difference between them in method and approach. By way of illustration, two representative writers of this period can be cited: Pope Innocent IV, the great canonist, and Alexander of Hales, the respected Franciscan theologian.

Innocent IV, in his *Apparatus in quinque libros decretalium* (c. 1245), distinguishes between civil wars and "real" wars, that is, wars waged by independent princes against "strangers." In his discussion of this latter kind of war, he implies that the political community has certain rights defined in law which, if violated, require a prince to go to war. Innocent justifies such recourse to war to defend legal rights. In addition, included in his view of war as a penal sanction is the notion of war as an act of vindicative justice, a position reminiscent of Augustine.[8] Alexander of Hales deals with the question of just war in part 2 of book 3 of his *Summa theologica,* written in 1245. His discussions, too, constantly invoke Augustine, and as his citations clearly indicate, he believes that war is a justified punishment for the morally guilty.[9] These views corresponded to those of other representative thinkers of the period. Although a tendency to view war as a matter of violated legal rights was beginning to gain popularity, primarily among the canonists, the ancient Augustinian principle of war as a punishment for moral wickedness was still retained, most notably by theologians. Though the canonists significantly developed and sharpened important points, the philosophical and ethical defense of innocent immunity was chiefly accomplished by the theologians. Thus the dominant theological intellect of St. Thomas Aquinas presents itself as the culminating formulation of the medieval Christian notion of just war.

Any discussion of specific theories of Aquinas must be undertaken with caution. As with other syncretic thinkers, from Plato and Aristotle to Hegel and Marx, an analysis of a particular notion or position suffers when it is extracted from the entire corpus of their thought, taking it out of context. Yet there would be little point to a lengthy review of a content so vast. Suffice it to say that on war and killing, Aquinas was consistent with his system, and for his time his formulation was definitive. Unlike Augustine, who not only synthesized much previous tradition but also made profoundly original contributions, Thomas did not depart substantially from the tradition he inherited. In terms of just war theory, Thomas's work might be described as a "resynthesis."

Thomas takes up the problem of war in question 40 of his *Summa theologica, secunda secundae.*[10] The discussion is in four "articles," which deal with 1) the lawfulness of war; 2) if clerics are permitted to fight; 3) if ambushes and deceits are permitted; and 4) if it is lawful to fight on holy days.

He answers the first article and the question it poses by stating three conditions that must be fulfilled to make a war just. Just war must be declared by the properly constituted public authority; it must be provoked by a just cause; and finally, it must be governed by right intention. The key to Thomas's view of the nature and purpose of just war is contained in his remarks on the fulfillment of the first and second conditions. After denying the right of the private individual to wage war, he says:

> And as the care of the common weal is committed to those who are in authority, it is lawful for them to have recourse to the sword in defending that common weal against internal disturbances, when they punish evil-doers, according to the words of the Apostle (Rom. XIII.4): "He beareth not the sword in vain: for he is God's minister, an avenger to execute wrath upon him that doeth evil"; so, too, it is their business to have recourse to the sword of war in defending the common weal against external enemies.[11]

It is evident here that for Aquinas, as much as for Augustine on whom he relies, just war is a punishment for wickedness. To leave no doubt, he next quotes Augustine's definition of just war in arguing his own second condition of just cause.

> Wherefore Augustine says (Q. X., super Jos.): "A just war is wont to be described as one that avenges wrongs, when a nation or state has to be punished, for refusing to make amends for the wrongs inflicted by its subjects, or to restore what it has seized unjustly."[12]

Augustine is Aquinas's unquestioned authority, to the absolute exclusion of every other writer. Thomas employs here the Augustinian definition, transmitted to him through Gratian. However, Gratian had cited the definitions of both Sts. Isidore and Augustine. Thomas passes over Isidore's definition without mention, and also ignores the work of the canonists St. Raymond of Pennafort, Henry of Ostia ("Hostiensia"), and Innocent IV. Isidore's works were a major source of Roman law definitions, which were in turn incorporated into the works of the canon lawyers. St. Raymond and Henry of Ostia specifically quoted and accepted Isidore's definition of just war as later incorporated in Gratian. Thomas himself quoted Isidore numerous times, and was himself influenced by Roman law. When all these factors are balanced, the conclusion must be that Thomas purposely avoided Isidore's definition of just war, and also the partially re-fined definitions of the canon lawyers who followed Isidore. The reason for Thomas's preference is clear from his argument.

The element of war as a punishment for moral wrongdoing in Thomas's statements is too obvious to escape notice. Before citing St. Augustine's definition of just war, he remarks that "secondly, a just cause is required, namely that those who are attacked, should be attacked because they deserve it on account of some fault."[13] Add to this his constant use of definitions and observations from Augustine and it becomes clear to what a marked degree he subscribed to the Augustinian attitude. In the reply to objection 2, which denies the permissibility of war, Thomas argues that defense of the common good may require a man to use force, and verifies his statement by quoting Augustine's letter to Marcellinus:

> "For when we are stripping a man of the lawlessness of sin, it is good for him to be vanquished, since nothing is more hopeless than the happiness of sinners, whence arises a guilty impunity and an evil will, like an internal enemy."[14]

In reference to the necessity of a right intention, Thomas cites the following statement.

> "True religion looks upon as peaceful those wars that are waged not for motives of aggrandisement, or cruelty, but with the object of securing peace, *of punishing evil-doers,* and of uplifting the good."[15] (Italics added)

Thus Aquinas was following the clearly defined attitude of Augustine on the punitive nature of war.[16] In Thomas's view, war is not only a means of restoring a just peace but also a means by which the morally guilty (Augustine's "wicked men") may be punished. Because of their moral guilt as individuals, these persons in a real sense "merit" punishment. From this it could be concluded that Thomas in no way deviates from the "pure" Augustinian attitude that just war necessarily involves a punishment of the wicked for their wickedness.

The initial impression of this view is of dogmatic harshness. On this basis one could justify a fanatical attitude toward the enemy's presumed injustice and liability to punishment. Though in practice this was likely to be the effect, to Thomas the reverse should be true. His concern with the subjective guilt of the enemy should have a salutary effect because the implication is that few wars will actually meet his requirements: A belligerent must have certain knowledge of the subjective (intentional) guilt of an enemy; the commission of an unjust act is not sufficient proof that the act was committed with full intent, which alone would create moral guilt. According to the strict Augustinian-Thomistic view, then, theoretically, very few wars could be just.

Of what real importance is this other than to point up Thomas's agreement with Augustine, and his tacit disagreement with the slight modifications of the Augustinian doctrine that the canonists had introduced? It was noted earlier that the canonists relied on Isidore for their definition of just war. Isidore's definition included, as a subtle addition to Augustine's formulation, a clear indication that war may be justified to recover stolen goods. The implication of this addition did not escape the canonists, whose inheritance from Isidore included the Roman law. It pointed to a notion of objective, material rights to which a "state" was entitled and in defense or for recovery of which war might be justified. This juridical notion, when amplified and refined, tended to shift the emphasis from a consideration of the subjective intent and moral guilt of the enemy to an emphasis on the objective injustice of the enemy's act. The notion of punishment was not excluded, but it was definitely subordinated to the view that stressed the objective legal order as the criterion for judging when a right had been violated.[17]

There were two consequences of this less subjective and more juridically objective view of determining when a war may be just. In its final form, as spelled out by the writers of late scholasticism, this view could serve to justify more wars than the strict Augustinian-Thomistic view, since the subjective guilt of the enemy need no longer be considered; it was sufficient justification for a state to wage war if its legal rights had been violated. However, with the possibility of more wars being justified another consequence would follow: specific rules had to be established to guarantee that these more frequent wars would be conducted justly. The more limited the theoretical justification for war, the less attention was given to the conduct of war; the broader the theoretical justification, the greater the concern to limit the conduct. Thomas consciously turns his back on the nascent juridical view being developed by the canonists in favor of the far stricter Augustinian doctrine, which, if adhered to rigidly, could justify few wars.

Thomas's subscription to the moral and punitive notion of war is perhaps one reason why he, like Augustine, did not concern himself with the question of a war's proper conduct. As Bede Jarrett has observed,

> Already everyone was sure that fighting was lawful to a Christian; but this common knowledge and practice was difficult to fit in with the rest of Christian teaching. Thus most of the problems of the thirteenth century were problems of thought and not of conduct.[18]

Essentially, Thomas did not come to grips completely with the reality of war in all its practical aspects. As a theologian, he was still concerned to square the existence of war ("This great physical evil"—Augustine) with Christian love. Thomas was not dealing with war in the abstract only; however, as a speculative theologian, he was more concerned with the morality of war in general than with the specifics of its conduct. His more speculative concern, coupled with his choice of an attitude that would allow few wars, partly explains his failure to consider the ethics of war's conduct. Thomas seemed strangely oblivious to contemporary custom and thought, which was concerned with the proper conduct of war. It is obvious that neither the customary limitations on war, such as the Peace of God, which had developed since Augustine's time, nor the work of the canon and civil lawyers had any influence on him. In this respect, at least, it can be concluded that Thomas was not a man of his time.

His real contribution to the developing theoretical notion of innocent immunity within a just war structure cannot be gleaned from his arguments on the conditions of just cause (*jus ad bellum*) but rather from his position on justified homicide. It is not surprising that Thomas should entertain the same doubts as had Augustine on the matter of private self-defense:

Suchlike precepts, as Augustine observes (*De Serm. Dom. in Monte* i.), should always be borne in readiness of mind, so that we be ready to obey them, and, if necessary, to refrain from resistance or self-defense.[19]

"Nevertheless," he concludes, "it is necessary sometimes for a man to act otherwise for the common good, or for the good of those with whom he is fighting."[20]

Thomas here seems to be as rigid in his denial of self-defense as was Augustine, only permitting one man to kill another for public safety. This is not the case, however.[21] For Thomas's complete view, his argument on the question "Whether it is lawful to kill a man in self-defense?" must be considered. At the same time considering the possibility of an act having two effects, he makes his position clear. His answer to the question as posed is worth quoting at length.

Nothing hinders one act from having two effects, only one of which is intended, while the other is beside the intention. Now moral acts take their species according to what is intended, and not according to what is beside the intention, since this is accidental as explained above (Q.XLIII., A.3: 1.-II., A. I., A. 3 a. 3). Accordingly, the act of self-defense may have two effects, one is the saving of one's life, the other is the slaying of the aggressor. Therefore, this act, since one's intention is to save one's own life, is not unlawful, seeing that it is natural to everything to keep itself in "being," as far as possible. And yet, though proceeding from a good intention, an act may be rendered unlawful, if it be out of proportion to the end. Wherefore if a man, in self-defense, uses more than necessary violence, it will be lawful, because according to the jurists, "it is lawful to repel force by force, provided one does not exceed the limits of a blameless defense." Nor is it necessary for salvation that a man omit the act of moderate self-defense in order to avoid killing the other man, since one is bound to take more care of one's own life than of another's. But as it is unlawful to take a man's life except for the public authority acting for the common good, as stated above (A.3), it is not lawful for a man to intend killing a man in self-defense, except for such as have public authority, who while intending to kill a man in self-defense, refer this to the public good, as in the case of a soldier fighting against the foe, and in the minister or the judge struggling with robbers, although even these sin if they be moved by private animosity.[22]

This is a remarkable statement, so pregnant with meaning that it deserves the closest scrutiny. Thomas has qualified Augustine's view on the permissibility of private self-defense. He is in complete agreement with Augustine that "it is not lawful for a man to intend killing a man in self-defense," but, whereas Augustine demanded omission of even the effort of self-defense, Thomas says explicitly, "Nor is it necessary for salvation that a man omit the act of moderate self-defense in order to avoid killing the other man. . . ." One may not kill an unjust aggressor directly, that is, intentionally, but may use proportional means to save one's own life even though these means may result in the death of the aggressor.

The striking disparity should be noted here between the views of Augustine and Aquinas. Augustine denied to an individual the action of self-defense because such action demonstrated an inordinate attachment to life, which he said was wrong, since one does not wholly own his body or his life. Yet Thomas clearly justified the permissibility of an act of moderate self-defense on grounds that "one is bound to take more care of one's own life than of another's."

Another feature of importance included in Thomas's discussion is his position on killing in war. Here again he is consistent with Augustine's views, maintaining that it is lawful for those who have public authority to intend to kill another "who while intending to kill a man in self-defense, refer this to the public good, as in the case of a soldier fighting against the foe." Thomas refers his readers back to article 3 of the present question, in which he states that

It is lawful to kill an evil doer in so far as it is directed to the welfare of the whole community, so that it belongs to him alone who has charge of the community's welfare. Thus it belongs to a physician to cut off a decayed limb, when he has been entrusted with the care of the health of the whole body. Now the care of the common good is entrusted to persons of rank having public authority: wherefore they alone, and not private individuals, can lawfully put evil doers to death.[23]

The important point here is Thomas's opinion that it is permissible to kill the enemy directly, that is, with intent. The only necessary qualification is that the person who kills with public authority refer his actions as a means to the end of the public good. The soldier cannot kill from a motive of private vengeance or animosity but must will that his actions serve the common good. Aquinas in this respect does not add anything to Augustine's position, but he does state unequivocally what Augustine had implied but hesitated to state as clearly: The enemy may be killed directly as a means to the end of preserving or defending the common good. This notion includes the assumption that the soldier, as in the case of the judge, is visiting just punishment on wicked men who merit death.

Finally, the most important notion contained in Thomas's discussion of the lawfulness of self-defense is his enunciation of a principle that was to have profound effect on the concept of innocent immunity in wartime. The sentence that begins "Nothing hinders one act from having two effects" has been called the historical beginning of the notion of double effect as a principle of moral reasoning.[24]

The principle of "double effect" had been employed by moralists for some time. Though an invaluable aid to solving many moral questions, its apparent theoretical simplicity tends to disguise the difficulties that can arise in its practical application. In its modern form, the principle's theoretical conditions are clear enough, yet when it is applied to a concrete case it is difficult to determine accurately whether, in fact, these conditions are fulfilled to the degree that would allow the action. In its contemporary formulation, the principle of "double effect" includes four conditions that must be verified simultaneously before a person may perform an action that will have both a good and an evil effect: 1) the action in terms of its object must be good in itself or at least indifferent; 2) one must intend only the good effect, not the evil effect; 3) the good effect must not be produced by the evil effect;

and 4) there must be a proportionately grave reason for permitting the evil effect. It is the determination of what constitutes a "sufficiently grave reason" that is troublesome.[25]

After all the texts are sifted, Thomas's position appears to be that one may not intend to kill an attacker in private self-defense; but, with public authority, the death of an unjust man may be willed directly, though only as a means to achieve some public good.

The final element in this scenario is Thomas's view on killing the innocent. In question 64 he answers the question of whether it is ever lawful to kill the innocent with the unequivocal statement, "It is in no way lawful to slay the innocent."[26] But if this statement is weighed in the measure of his "double effect" arguments, one can only conclude that what Thomas intends to prohibit is the direct or intentional killing of the innocent. Therefore accidental or unintended death is not sinful.

With hindsight it is easy to conclude that there are serious shortcomings in Thomas's argument. For example, why does he confine his arguments to the moral sphere, with no attention to the legal? Why does he seemingly ignore the practical customary immunity of noncombatants? And, flowing from these omissions, why does he not consider the matter of objective fault, or "crime," and concentrate instead on the traditional subjective moral guilt of those involved in bloodshed? Thomas, with all his genius, could not transcend the rarified philosophical and theological issues that preoccupied him. He built on the work of his predecessors and he built well, but the resulting construction, at least as concerned the innocent in wartime, is incomplete. It is ironic that more humble intellects, indebted in large measure to him, would see paths that he did not and, being more sensitive to the realities of human suffering, would follow those paths to their ends.

The innocents' debt to Aquinas is indirect but nevertheless profound. His principle of double effect provided a tool of moral reasoning that later thinkers could incorporate, with all its imperfections, into a new examination of the *jus in bello*. With Thomas, the last word had been spoken to rationalize the just offensive war. The theological tradition begun with Augustine had now reached its apex. The next step was to analyze warfare and killing with a perspective much broader than the theological one, to incorporate the parallel work of the secular lawyers, and thus to consider the problem of public conflict in all its dimensions.

With the disintegration of Roman authority and the resultant political anarchy, it is understandable that scholars should turn to that seemingly last remaining continuum with the past, the structure of Roman law, as an anchor in a very troubled social sea. The Code of Justinian, the first part of which, the *Digest,* was published in 533 A.D., constituted the juristic base for Western Europe throughout the Middle Ages. A group of trained intellectuals arose who assumed the task of explaining with addenda or "glosses" the texts of Roman law. They came to be called the "Glossators" or "civilian" lawyers (so called to distinguish them from the clerical or canon lawyers), and they concerned themselves with the editing of and commentary on the traditional legal edicts and principles. But the conditions of life in medieval Europe were far different from those that obtained when Justinian's Code was published. Adaptation obviously was required and was provided by a second generation of commentators, a group of scholars known to historians as the "Post-Glossators." Foremost among them were Cyrus, Bartolus, Baldus, and Lucas de Penna.[27]

Born about 1320 in Naples, Lucas de Penna was highly respected by his fellow jurists and his later influence was felt far beyond his native land, while he was himself greatly influenced by the philosophy and theology of his own time. Lucas was a secular jurist who embodied in his thought both the sacred and profane traditions. Modern warfare is closely linked with international law, which in turn rests on an assumption of the existence of sovereign, independent states; these did not exist in modern form at the time of Lucas, and it is therefore somewhat surprising that he demonstrates as much concern as he does for the legal determinations affecting war among states.

According to Lucas, the criteria that render a war unjust, in spite of the fulfillment of certain legal premises by the belligerents, are of both an objective and a subjective nature, corresponding to the cause for which war is waged, and to the intention of the belligerents. Examples of a just cause of war are retribution for wrongs inflicted, the repelling of invasions, the recovery of goods illegally or unjustly seized, and a surprising new justification, the securing of liberty, which is the "most just" cause. But even if the cause is just, an evil intention on the part of the belligerents renders the war unjust. Such evil intention includes the lust for power or domination, the desire to wage war for the sake of revenge, and a vindictive desire to cause the enemy unnecessary harm. The influence of the Augustinian-Thomistic theological tradition is too obvious to require further comment.

On the proper conduct of war, Lucas is explicit. In war, the belligerents are not at liberty to act without restraint. Soldiers may not be given license to murder, rob, plunder, rape, or constrain civilians; those who do such things should be as severely punished as if the crimes had been committed in peacetime. Once the enemy has been captured and is therefore incapable of doing further harm, he should be treated humanely.[28] Since the aim of just war is peace ("Bellum geritur, ut pax acquiratur"),[29] those responsible should be aided so that peaceful intercourse between the societies can be restored as quickly as possible. Lucas's view of the enemy rests upon the premise that there are individuals among them who should not be injured or held responsible for the acts of their fellow citizens. Active participation in injustice now becomes the criterion for judging the guilty among the enemy.

Lucas contends that reprisals can only be taken against the guilty members of a "corporation." "Since only a certain number of individuals are guilty of wrongs, it is against the principle of justice and equity to extend their liability to their innocent fellow members."[30] Applying this principle to the *civitas,* Lucas concludes that only those who partake in or countenance the wrong actions of the ruler may be held responsible for those actions: "Contra personas singulares, quae non deliquerunt, nullo modo repressaliae concedi possunt."[31]

Lucas's views show to what extent the civilian jurists of the period after St. Thomas addressed themselves to the concrete problems of war's conduct. Lucas is an excellent example of a nontheologian who nevertheless viewed war primarily in its moral and philosophical dimensions, while at the same time laying down practical legal rules that were seen as based on these moral premises. Though imbued with the Augustinian-Thomistic moral tradition of war, his juridical bent led him to see that war is capable of both juridical and moral limitation. And because the prime matter of law is objective fact, Lucas saw that the first consideration of guilt must be through concrete act or *delict*. Those who did not participate in the unjust action could not be held responsible for it. In war, therefore, those innocent of the *delict*—most obviously the civilians, but even soldiers whose aggressive actions had been ended—should be spared.

These views were perhaps not then shared by all jurists, but they did eventually prevail. Because of this, Lucas must be ranked as a major thinker who contributed greatly to the development of the principle of noncombatant immunity.

Part II
Customary Origins

V Medieval Warfare and Its Limitations

With heart and prowess the Franks have stood; slain was the heathen multitude; of a hundred thousand survive not two: The archbishop crieth, "Oh staunch and true! Written it is in the Frankish geste, that our Emperor's vassals shall bear them best."

The Song of Roland

The Emperor came on: a dawn of spears darker than night rose over the leaguered city.

The Monk of St. Gall

In tracing the emergence of the idea—and ultimately the law— of civilian immunity, the emphasis has been on the theories of great thinkers in antiquity and the early Middle Ages. The impression might be that their ideas developed in a vacuum, because Augustinian-Thomistic just war theory seemed oblivious to contemporary institutions and military practice. This impression is not entirely false. One of the ironies of civilian immunity is that the elements of its composition sprang from intellectual and practical sources that paralleled each other yet rarely coalesced, and only finally firmly combined at the time of the Renaissance. Just as Christian just war theory provided the philosophical grounds of innocent immunity—that is, the matrix from which finally evolved a generalized notion of moral innocence in war—so, too, legal and social institutions emerged that would in their turn provide the basis for a notion of objective nonparticipation in war. Civilian immunity owes as much to this latter development as it does to the former.

One of the most important social influences was a simple humanitarian reaction to the pitiless bloodshed and social insecurity that characterized Europe with the disintegration of the Roman Empire. This impulse was to cause an articulate demand from all classes of society for some limitations to and protection from the ravages of private and feudal wars. Its climax was manifested in such movements as the Peace of God and the codes of medieval chivalry. These institutions signaled the start of a new era, yet were born from the feudal military and social fabric of the Dark Ages. From the chaos and gloom of that period, from the anarchy and brutality that so commonly invested the lives of its people, a new order developed. With the beauty and dignity in the art and manners of the High Middle Ages came a greater appreciation of the dignity of every person. With this appreciation came greater control over violence.

The essential factor that accounted for the rise of feudalism was the need for protection. For centuries, the masses of western Europe under Roman domination and protection had been pacified and rendered unwarlike. The professional armies of Rome provided all necessary protection of life and property. With the disintegration of the western Roman Empire as an effective political organization, under centuries of invasion-migrations, security vanished. Later, the conquest of Syria, Egypt, North Africa, and Spain by the Moslems appeared to be only a prelude to the fate of all Europe. Though the Moslem threat was turned back by Charles Martel at Tours in 732, that threat lingered, only to be joined by a far greater menace from the north.[1]

The first recorded Viking raid occurred in 799, but forays did not become large in scale until the middle of the ninth century. Western Europe lost the limited defensive capability of Charlemagne's armies when his empire was politically and militarily fragmented after his death in 814. Against the Vikings, a commentator has observed that

> Europe had no adequate defenses for several decades. The old Frankish general levy was too slow and ponderous to cope with these elusive foemen, the peasantry too poorly trained and armed. The only sound military remedies were to be found in the principles left by Charlemagne—fortification, mailed cavalry, fewer and better soldiers.[2]

Finally, a remedy was found by reorganizing western Christendom as a defensive fortress. The decisive time was the ninth century and the program was the body of military principles of conduct and organization inherited from Charlemagne. The result was feudalism.[3]

There are two senses in which the term "feudalism" is generally used: in a restricted sense it refers to the legal relationships among fiefs and fiefholders; in a more general sense, it refers to the sociopolitical fabric of the Middle Ages.[4] Here both meanings are included, since the distinction is not important for an understanding of the feudal-military relationship. The Carolingian principles of military organization and conduct were fully developed by the tenth century. The military origins of feudalism, however, began with Charlemagne's grandfather, Charles Martel. Charles Martel needed an effective permanent fighting force to stabilize his power. Since there was little money, but land was plentiful, Charles employed a system of endowing land grants, called "benefices," on his warriors, a device the Catholic Church had used for some time.[5]

Germanic custom had long recognized the existence of a body of personal retainers who owed personal allegiance to the chief, the *comitatus,* or trustee, and were bound to their lord by a special oath.[6] Charles Martel combined this institution with the benefice. "The men to whom he gave benefices swore to be ever faithful to him. As the term *vassus* was in common use for dependents of various kinds, Charles applied it to his new soldiers. They became *vassi dominici,* vassals of the lord."[7] The practice spread and was copied by great lords who in turn granted benefices from their proprietary lands. With the dissipation of central authority after Charlemagne's death, this practice remained one of the few stabilizing factors in society, providing a nucleus of loyal warriors who were almost completely self-sufficient.

The essence of the feudal relationship was a series of vertically ascending and descending agreements between lords and vassals. These hierarchical allegiances, gradually institutionalized as experience hardened into custom, and providing for grants of land in exchange for the mutual agreement by lord and vassal to protect and serve each other, constituted the feudal system.

It is true that "as a political system, pure feudalism was little removed from anarchy."[8] Nevertheless, primitive as it was, it was a step removed and, serving its purpose, was the first slow lurch toward the ultimate reorganization of a more comprehensive and stable political order. It is interesting to note that "pure feudalism" existed in the west Frankish state (modern France) to a much greater degree than in the east Frankish state (modern Germany). The reason for this was that in the tenth and eleventh centuries the east Frankish state was ruled by strong kings who resisted the pressure of fief subdivision with its consequent dilution of allegiance to the ultimate lord, the king, and instead retained the original notion of fiefs granted directly from the king. In short, feudalism presented many faces, each one depending on locale, custom, and the challenge of circumstances. Some general features did persist, however, regardless of variations.

At the heart of the feudal system was the fully armed warrior, the knight, the *miles,* the warrior of excellence. The feudal contract bound the lord to protect his vassal, his family, and his fief, in return for which the knight owed military service and certain civil obligations. On call, the knight was expected to appear with such retainers as were necessary to make him effective as a fighting man. Fortifying his home (*castellum*, or little fort), he became locally impregnable, and had his own vassals upon whom he himself could call in time of need. It was this person, assembling under threat, who finally repulsed the Vikings and brought to Christian Europe security from external attack.[9]

Although external danger diminished for Christian Europe as a whole, the problem of protecting Christians from each other remained ever-present and vexing. The very fact that feudal society was organized on the basis of vertical contracts tended to weaken further a remote and already weak central political authority. The reason for this is obvious: a vassal had certain obligations to his lord and to his own vassals, yet he had virtually no obligations to anyone else. "Outside the bounds of feudal custom, the vassal was unrestrained."[10] In this primitive political structure there existed very little control over the use of military force. Though secure from outside attack, European society was thoroughly insecure internally.

The lack of centralized or institutional control was the condition that permitted the real cause of internal insecurity to operate. By far the most disturbing element in early medieval feudal society was private feudal war.

> It assumed a more-or-less permanent state of war. While it provided machinery for the peaceful settling of most disputes, it did not compel men to settle their disputes peacefully. Thus if two knights quarreled, they could always find a feudal court competent to hear the case, but if they preferred to wage war on each other, and usually did, feudal custom did not hinder them.[11]

The right to settle a dispute by force of private arms was deeply ingrained in the custom of old Germanic law.[12] Any crime was considered a *Friedensbruch,* a rupture of the peace; the execution of a sanction against the wrongdoer was the *faida* or, in German, *Fehde.* The bonds of kinship permitted the kinsman of a victim to carry out this sanction himself if he so desired, especially when the *Friedensbruch* was homicide.[13]

This custom of ancient Germanic law became firmly rooted in feudal custom, even though as early as Charlemagne decrees were explicitly directed against it. In 802 Charlemagne expressly forbade private war; but with his death there passed the single authority capable of overriding immemorial custom. His successors were too weak to carry on his work; their authority was weak since obligations were commonly taken as personal, not institutional. Thus ancient custom prevailed.[14] Private feudal war flourished. The Church had always contested this right, but its influence, too, was reduced by the fact that many bishops were also fighting lords. Not until the clergy received the articulated support of the masses were gains made in the attempt to limit private feudal war.[15]

The Middle Ages was the period of the "cavalry cycle." From a military standpoint, cavalry supremacy was the most important characteristic of medieval combat.[16] The great historian of medieval warfare, Sir Charles Oman, considers its period to ex-

tend from the defeat of the Emperor Valens at Adrianople in 387
to the destruction of English feudalism in the Wars of the Roses,
which ended in 1485; the period from Adrianople to the battle
of Hastings in 1066 is the period of cavalry development; the
period after Hastings is the era of the knight's unchallenged
supremacy. Just as appropriately, this span of eleven hundred
years can also be called the era of fortification, for the building
of walled cities and fortresses was equally a mark of the age. These
two features, the mailed or armored knight, and the fortified
town or castle, characterized both the military tactics and mentality of the Middle Ages, for both were fundamentally in-
struments of defense.

As a victory of the Gothic cavalry over the degenerate Roman
infantry legions, Adrianople was a sign of times to come. In this
battle, in which the Emperor Valens died with all his chief officers and forty thousand men, heavy cavalry had demonstrated
its ability to annihilate even the heavy infantry of Rome. The
Goth "had become the arbiter of war, the lineal ancestor of all
the knights of the Middle Ages, the inaugurator of that ascendency
of the horseman which was to endure for a thousand years."[17]
Near the end of the fourth century, the restless Gallic legions of
Rome rose in revolt against Theodosius. But he had learned well
the lesson of Adrianople and completely reorganized the troops
of the eastern Empire. He abandoned the traditional Roman
reliance on infantry and instead made his cavalry the most important part of the imperial army. The rebels were soundly
defeated by the Emperor's armies at Frigidus in 387. As a result,
cavalry became as important in the west as in the east.

The history of the later Roman Empire in the west reveals the
rapid adoption of cavalry techniques. At the battle of Chalons
in 450 the Visigothic cavalry, allied to Aetius and his Romans,
defeated the Huns in a chiefly cavalry engagement. In the east,
always ahead of the west in military technique, the great Belisarius
not only preserved Justinian's Empire against the horsemen of
Asia but, in his campaign against the Goths, used armed horse
archers and proved the superiority of an integrated fighting
force.[18]

It is remarkable that lessons so painfully learned should be so easily forgotten. With the disintegration of Rome as a military power, the Franks inherited the task of defending Europe, first against the Moors and later against the Avars and Vikings. The Franks were long in acquiring the use of the horse in battle and had to learn by trial and error lessons that had already been mastered by the late Romans; but once they did they became invincible. Of Frankish tactics prior to Charlemagne, it has been stated that

> The use of the horse in battle seems to extend itself in exactly the same proportion as that of body armour, spreading downward through the sixth and seventh centuries, till, by the close of the Merovingian age, it has become usual among the upper classes; the counts and dukes with their immediate retinues were habitually fighting on horseback by the end of the seventh century, though when pressed or surrounded they would still dismount and fight on foot like their ancestors.[19]

Though cavalry and armor were beginning to replace the horde armed with clubs and spears, there was nothing in the Merovingian army organization to suggest the future feudal levy.

Charlemagne sought to replace the old Frankish *leveé en masse* of ill-disciplined and poorly armed infantry with a smaller, better disciplined and heavily armed cavalry. The *Capitulare de exercitu promovendo* of 803 commanded all great vassals to take the field when summoned with a specified number of armed retainers, the number of men and types of equipment to depend upon the size of the landholdings of the lord. These and supplementary requirements were included in four later decrees. One of the results was to concentrate military obligation, interest, and training in the aristocratic class, relieving the poorer classes of freemen from such duty. As the feudal system spread, the number of freemen declined as the vassal-lord relationship was extended downward. The poor foot soldier, who could not afford expensive equipment, was steadily reduced in his auxiliary status, with a correspondingly increased emphasis on the mailed knight, who was of necessity a wealthy lord.

Historians of this period agree that the most important of Charlemagne's innovations was his systematic use of fortified posts. In order to maintain his control over subject regions, he set up a series of palisaded posts called "burgs" in districts of strategic importance. These forts were picketed by a garrison and were used as pivot points for his mobile cavalry forces. Another innovation (or revival of ancient usage) was the supply train for extended campaigns.[20]

The two military principles of armored cavalry and strategic fortification came to dominate western Europe. Though the central organization for implementing them disappeared with Charlemagne's death, about when the new threat to security appeared in the form of the Vikings, the ideas were still at hand. So, too, was the new method of implementation in the form of the feudal system. The welding together of all these elements was to produce the knightly society whose aristocratic champions were to cause so much chaos with their private feuds.

The climax of cavalry supremacy was the battle of Hastings in 1066. In this daylong melee the English infantry acquitted itself with courage. Armed with axes, King Harold's men out-fought the invading Norman infantry. But the English were forced to fight defensively because they could not match the mobility of the Norman knights. As a result they were subjected to the devastating missile fire of William's archers and finally decimated by the repeated charges of the Norman heavy cavalry. Contemporary chroniclers credited the victory to the cavalry, although the casualties and confusion caused by the infantry archers were an equally deciding factor. Many future battles would be lost when infantry archers were not used to support cavalry. But this lesson escaped notice, and as a result of the credit given the armored knight, "within a generation the heavy armed foot soldier practically disappeared from Europe except in remote Slavic and Scandinavian regions."[21]

The mailed rider became everywhere supreme, dominating his world politically as well as militarily.

Now for the only time in history we find a single human being, the mounted man-at-arms, functioning virtually as a combat unit. Summed up in his iron-clad person were the destinies of a feudal tract of land, tilled by sullen serfs and depending for its defense upon his unimaginative tactics.[22]

Infantry was to fall into such disregard that its battle losses were seldom considered important enough to mention. For centuries the knight ruled battles unmolested. In the words of one commentator, the state of the unmounted fighting man is an index to the social conditions of an age:

> When men are slumbering, careless or brutalized, it [the infantry] is abject and despised; and it only shows what it is capable of when privilege and inequality have been replaced by a social system which pays more attention to the dignity of man.[23]

To an extent, however, the social and economic structure of medieval warfare itself acted as a restraint on the conduct of war. While the general population was not immune, the number of combatants was relatively small. To be a noble was to be a mounted soldier, a prerequisite that only a tiny portion of the population could meet; similarly, the prestige and other gains of combat lay in defeating another knight.

The economy of feudal Europe was predominantly agricultural; commerce was mostly barter. Taxation was practically nonexistent. To equip himself and finance even a minor campaign, a knight needed serfs who were skilled artisans—who were few—or he needed some form of wealth. Few landowners could afford to be warriors. The effective weapons of the period required early training and constant practice. These were also luxuries that only a few could afford. The economic value of defeating another knight was therefore of prime importance—but not that of killing him: "If you killed a hostile knight his son owed you nothing but hatred. If you captured him he would buy his liberty with as large a sum as he could possibly raise. Accordingly it paid better to take prisoners than to kill."[24] Economic necessity tended to keep low the numbers who could afford to wage feudal war, while at the same time it provided a motive for such war. Yet this same necessity decreed that the most valuable knight was a live one. Once the enemy nobles were captured (or killed) there would commonly be little point on either side in continuing the fray.

There were other socioeconomic limitations on feudal war. A lord who was attacked could hold his vassals to their military obligations until the invader was repulsed; but a lord bent on offensive war could keep his men in the field for only forty days out of each year, after which they must be paid, a demand only a great lord could meet. The forty-day obligation also enhanced the value of having a strongly fortified castle to retire to. A stronghold often allowed a lesser vassal to defy his lord if he chose to, since few castles could be starved into submission or taken by siege within the time limit. As a consequence, few feudal wars were major wars in scale or duration, though violence was constant.

The lot of the noncombatant was hardly an easy or safe one. Subject to the whim, greed, or foraging of the warrior, his life and goods were in constant peril. But if no formal rules of immunity existed, and if in practice the ordinary, unarmed "civilian" often sustained depredations at the hands of the armed, nevertheless early feudal society did contain inner limits that reduced the ravages wrought on civilians. In the end the system, after filling a political and military vacuum, proved a capacity for future growth in the direction of limiting—but also of expanding—public conflict.

VI

The "Peace of God" and Chivalry

We command also that priests, clerics, monks, travelers, merchants, country people going and returning, and those engaged
in agriculture, as well as the animals with which they till the
soil . . . shall at all times be secure.

Canon XX, *Second Lateran Council*

Lo, behold the great evil adventure that fell that Saturday. For
they slew as many good prisoners as would well have been worth,
one with another, 400,000 francs.

The Chronicles of Froissart

The Dark Ages were not totally devoid of illumination but they
were deeply shrouded. Europe's history in this era reveals a society
largely bereft of order and at the mercy of rampant violence. Little
imagination is needed to appreciate what devastation early
medieval society suffered at the hands of warriors who claimed
the right to settle their private disputes by force. Most writers
consider the Middle Ages a period of "limited war" from the standpoint of the number of warriors involved. No one, however, could
consider the time from the fall of the western Roman Empire to
the twelfth century as an era of limited warfare in any but this
special sense.

Wars for the most part were short. Few persons were directly
engaged in the fighting, and for the warriors themselves the lure
of ransom often prevented death in defeat. But these facts did
not diminish the effects of feudal violence on the nonfighting
population, who often suffered terribly: monasteries and churches sacked, farms and villages burned and plundered. The peace
movements that originated in the tenth century sprang from the
nonwarrior classes. When medieval warfare is called limited,
therefore, it must be so understood in reference to the warfare

65

of the High Middle Ages. In large measure the mitigation of violence in that period was due directly to the influence of the tenth and eleventh century peace movements.

In the last years of the tenth century, a wave of popular protest against the unrestrained violence of private feudal war was channeled into a series of canonical decrees to which historians have given the names the Peace of God and the Truce of God. Though there were two separate movements involved, the Peace of God and the Truce of God are usually referred to in their later combined form as the Truce of God.[1] The basic difference between the two movements, aside from the times of their respective beginnings, lies in their aims. Though the intent of both was to limit private feudal wars, the one sought to limit the impact of war on persons and things, while the other attempted to limit war's duration. The Peace of God was designed to protect certain classes and their possessions, thus limiting legitimate objects of attack. The Truce of God, on the other hand, sought to limit the incidence of war, not by prohibiting it entirely but by restricting it to specified periods of time and seasons of the year. The Peace of God, as a formal movement, antedated the Truce of God, though its prescriptions were later tacitly assumed to be included in the Truce. Hence the formal distinction tended to disappear as time went on. Here the concern is with the formal prescriptions of the Peace of God and its later influence on custom and practice.[2]

In 988, at the monastery of Charroux in Poitou, a Church council was held, attended by numerous clerics and laymen. One of the avowed objects of the council was to discuss the problems caused by incessant private war. The assembled members hoped to find some means of exerting their influence on the bellicose feudal nobility to cease their warlike activities. Canon I declared that those who violated churches would be anathema; Canon II pronounced the same sanction on those who pillaged the poor; and Canon III condemned those who attacked an unarmed cleric.[3] With this statement, signed by the Archbishop of Bordeaux and the Bishops of Poitiers, Limoges, Perigueux, Saintes, and Angoulême, the unarticulated wishes of so many among the clergy and laity became a sharply defined rule and guiding principle. The peace movement had begun, and under the leadership and authority of the Church it was to spread rapidly. "The Council of Charroux marks the emergence of a vague collective consciousness that was to soon crystallize in a widespread public movement of unusual social idealism. It definitely introduced the first wave of popular enthusiasm for peace in pre-crusading France."[4]

The object of the Council of Charroux and later French councils was not to outlaw war or even to restrict its duration. The aim was to limit the effects of war on the noncombatant portion of the population. Though expressing an idealism long foreign to European society, the Peace of God was actually very realistic. It attempted to formalize in rules the shared moral intuition that some members of the society ought not to suffer in wartime. The attempt to actualize this feeling by using the authority of the Church was perfectly reasonable, not only because it was the interpretive custodian of what was moral and immoral but because the Church was the one organization powerful enough to enforce some such rules of conduct. Though the Church's desire to alleviate war's ravages was no doubt based upon humanitarian motives, there were other, equally compelling reasons why it promoted peace. It was the greatest property owner, yet it did not have the physical resources to defend its properties from depredation. By fostering a peace policy and throwing the weight of its moral influence into the balance, with the implicit or actual threat that it would ally itself with those who supported this principle, the Church sought to protect itself as well as the other defenseless.

Under the influence of the Church, the spark that was struck at Charroux began to burn brightly in the south of France. In 990 a council was held at Narbonne, the first of several that were to affirm and define the status of noncombatants. This council declared against nobles who confiscated the goods of ecclesiastics and attacked their persons. The sanctions for transgressing these prescriptions were individual excommunication, with communal interdiction (the equivalent of excommunication or ostracism of the whole community) should it be determined that the immoral actions of a noble enjoyed the consent of his subjects. Under the auspices of Widon, Bishop of Prey, and of Theobald, Archbishop of Vienne, a written pact was entered into between the nobles and the bishops in 998, called the "Pact of Peace." Its provisions demanded protection of the weak, of laborers, and of merchants.[5] The south of France had given the signal for reform.

From its beginnings in local synods in the south and center of France the peace campaign spread north, to include all of France and eventually parts of Germany. It then swept south into Catalonia, where the civil authorities later formalized and enforced its rules.[6] In the second quarter of the eleventh century, the Peace of God reached its climax as an independent movement as the French began collectively to support the public cause. The next step was the formal blending of the Peace and Truce of God, which was accomplished at the Council of Elne in 1027. By this council it was forbidden to attack or slay unarmed clerics, men going to or coming from Church councils, and men escorting women. The penalty for such actions was excommunication.[7] Two peace councils were held at Narbonne, in 1043 and 1045. The canons of these councils are not extant but the peripheral evidence indicates that they reaffirmed allegiance to the principles of the Peace and Truce. The importance of these councils lies not only in the nature of their decrees, but also in the machinery which was being developed to deal with violations of the rules.

One of the most important French local synods was convened at Narbonne in 1054. At this synod the distinction between the Peace and Truce was still made. Hence Canons I through X refer specifically to the Truce, and Canons XI through XXIX to the Peace of God. In addition to the rules and prohibitions protecting the person and property of unarmed clerics and their companions from attack, the canons also prescribe that serfs and their property should enjoy equal protection. Six canons discuss the equal obligations of women to obey the terms of the Peace. Olive groves are also to be immune from attack but not for their agricultural value: the olive is the sign of peace and its oil is used for holy chrism.[8]

In this council occurs a statement that at once raises the peace movement, and the councils that were its expression, to a level above the mere pragmatic desire to safeguard life and property. Canon I says, "He who kills a Christian, without doubt sheds the blood of Christ."[9] Although the thought was implicit in the intentions of many who had fostered the peace movement since its inception, here finally was an explicit expression of the principle that the Christian must hold Christian life sacred for Christ's sake. Even though the defenseless who should be spared were still limited to "Christian," the importance of the explicit expression at the Council of Narbonne can hardly be overestimated.

A further step in the direction of extending immunity was marked by the Second Council of Elne in 1065. In its canons protection was extended to all domestic animals, and homicide of any sort was forbidden.

By this time, the influence of the French peace movement had permeated Catalonia to the southwest and Germany to the northeast. All that was required now was papal approval in order to consolidate the gains already made. It was not long in coming. In 1059, Pope Nicholas II issued a bull to all the bishops of Gaul stating that pilgrims would be immune from attack. Already at the Council of Rheims in 1049, Pope Leo IX had declared that clerics in holy orders and poor people should be immune. Finally, at Clermont in 1095, Pope Urban II's plea for subscription to the Truce of God threw the whole weight of the Church's authority behind these rules to limit war. Clermont has been correctly called not only the most important council of its time for the propagation of the Peace and Truce of God but also the most important in its effect on the next century. The crucial canons from this council are the first, thirtieth, and thirty-first. Canon I confirms immunity for clerics, monks, and women, while the other canons proscribe violence against the Church, and prescribe anathema against those who kill clerics or steal their goods. But of far greater importance are the twelve "peace decrees" of Urban II. The first seven decrees deal specifically with the principles of the Peace, while the last five pertain to the Truce. For the most part these decrees are a restatement of the ideas of earlier canons, but are here presented in great detail and over the signature of a pope. For the future, this is their importance.[10]

With clerical direction and papal approval, the Peace and Truce had become part of the public consciousness. One commentator has observed that the chief gain for society was the development of an active public opinion. "The peace movement fostered the development of public opinion in eleventh century France, and actually brought forth a distinctly new public conscience on matters concerned with law and order."[11]

The Truce of God, and by common understanding the Peace of God also, was reaffirmed without detailed comment at the first Lateran Council in 1123, and the Truce was reaffirmed at the Second and Third Lateran Councils in 1139 and 1179. It is a comment on the times, however, that these reaffirmations were necessary.

The Church had taken the initiative in promoting the peace movement for various reasons. One, as already noted, was that the secular political authority was incapable of limiting private war. Hence, almost by default, the Church assumed this responsibility. It is probable, too, that churchmen felt it their duty to promote protection of the weak and defenseless. One can understand, for example, why the Church would be concerned for the security of its pilgrims, since pilgrimages were commonly prescribed as a penance. Hence the Church might be expected to exert what pressure it could to protect the large numbers of Christians who embarked on a pilgrimage at its direction. At the same time, where a modicum of civil authority did exist, rulers were quick to incorporate the principles of the peace movement into law. One of the best examples can be found as early as 1061. From then to 1063 Count Ramon Berenguer promulgated the *Ustages de Barcelona*. This code was derived from an earlier code of the Emperor Lothair II and was an attempt to reconcile the practice of the old allodial system of property with the newer system of benefices and *honores*.[12] Among other provisions were those that set punishments for breaches of the Peace and Truce of God, and of various ecclesiastical pronouncements, one of which had decreed protection for the Jews. A later code, *Las siete partidas,* prepared between 1256 and 1263 but put into force only in 1348, included several chapters devoted to military rules and discipline. But this is already in a period of greater humanization of war when the results of the efforts exerted in the tenth and eleventh centuries had become evident.

Finally, no overview of the ways in which medieval society sought to limit private war would be complete without mention of the chivalric code. On the development of this knightly code, too, the Church's influence was great. Students of medieval chivalry make a distinction among three forms of knightly ethics: between feudal and religious chivalry, and between these types and romantic chivalry. The distinction is a valid one, but to understand the influence of chivalry on military conduct only the feudal and religious forms are important.

In citing the origins of the chivalric code it is necessary to reiterate the point already made with regard to the Peace of God: At its base there was an almost inextricable mixture of religious idealism and pragmatic intent, a desire on the one hand to Christianize the warrior in order to save his soul, combined with a desire to tame him in order to save the lives and property of the rest of the population.

In a feudal society, in which the aristocratic knight enjoyed such tremendous prestige, it is easy to understand how the virtues of military prowess—courage, skill, and above all loyalty to one's feudal lord—should come to be admired. When these virtues were channeled to the service of the Church, or at least restrained by an ethical ideal, the feudal warrior would become the Christian knight. The primary function of the feudal aristocracy was to fight; its secondary function was to provide some form of temporal government. The extent to which the Church exerted a civilizing influence on this fighting and governing class can scarcely be overestimated.

Before looking in greater detail at this civilizing process, it should be observed how the very factors accounting for the knight's military predominance also contributed to the development of a knightly code of action. The armored knight enjoyed supremacy for several reasons: noble birth, wealth, leisure, long training; and a "class which makes war both its vocation and avocation is bound to develop rules to alleviate its unpleasant features."[13] Since armor was heavy and hot, a knight wore it only when necessary. When he traveled, he carried his equipment on a pack horse. Hence, a custom soon developed requiring a knight to give his enemy time to don his armor before attacking him. Eventually, a knight could trust his fellow knight's word to such an extent that parole was commonly given for the vanquished knight to raise his ransom.[14]

Though such a code of military honor served the aristocratic warrior well in his relations with his peers, it did little of itself to alleviate the lot of the rest of the population, whose status placed it beyond the pale of knightly ethics. Only when the customs of feudal chivalry were infused with a religious idealism did a truly Christian ethic of knighthood appear. This fusion of ideals did not exist in a systematic form before the twelfth century, though its theoretical base goes back a century earlier.

The fundamental idea of religious chivalry was that a Christian knight, because of his power and privileged position, had obligations to defend the Church, its property and its flock, and to fulfill these obligations in accordance with ecclesiastical direction. This notion took root in the early crusades and was shaped into a definitive system by John of Salisbury. However, what is of importance here is not the final view of the Christian knight as the temporal protector of Christian society so much as the specific influence of the Church in developing this ideal. Here one encounters again the Peace of God, viewed this time not simply as a body of prohibitions but rather in its less definable form as an appeal to the warrior to become fully Christian, to assume the responsibility to protect the less privileged. By thus ennobling the warrior, elevating his military virtues instead of disparaging them, the Church was able to hope with some chance of success that its injunctions to limit war would be obeyed. Hence the code of the Christian warrior acted as a greater deterrent to the knight's lawless behavior than the threat of excommunication or exile. It became the duty of the knight *as a knight,* rather than just as a Christian, to obey the rules of the Peace. One who broke the Peace or ignored immunities was not only excluded from Christian society but, perhaps more significant, was considered outside the brotherhood of his peers. He became, in effect, déclassé, no knight at all.

The Church's effort to infuse this attitude into the knightly class is exemplified by two restrictions, apart from those of the Peace of God, which it attempted to impose on feudal war. On both counts it was unsuccessful, but the fact that the Church could even make the effort demonstrated the degree to which its influence had permeated the realm of knightly ethics before the end of the twelfth century. These restrictions applied to medieval tournaments and to the use of missile weapons.

By the twelfth century, the tournament, which had originated in northern France, was flourishing also in England and Germany. The tournaments of the twelfth century differed very little from actual battles. If life had grown dull in peacetime, a wealthy noble might arrange to hold a tourney. He would select a site and send out heralds to announce to all neighboring knights the time and place. On the appointed day the knights would assemble, choose sides, and put on their armor in safety zones. Then the two lines of heavy cavalry would charge each other. When lances were broken the combat would continue with swords and axes. Though the intent was not to kill but to force an opponent to yield so as to collect ransom, such "sport" was very dangerous and it is easy to see why the Church frowned on it.

The first ordinance directed against tournaments was Canon IX of the Synod of Clermont in 1130, of which the following canon from the Second Lateran Council (1139) is a repetition. It is worth citing in full.

> We condemn absolutely those detestable jousts or tournaments in which the knights usually come together by agreement and, to make a show of their strength and boldness, rashly engage in contests which are frequently the cause of death to men and of danger to souls. If anyone taking part in them should meet his death, though penance and the Viaticum shall not be denied him if he asks for them, he shall, however, be deprived of Christian burial.[15]

Even though stronger measures were urged at, for example, the
Fourth Lateran Council and the Council of Lyons, tournaments
continued to increase in popularity until the middle of the sixteenth century (though by this late date they had lost their former
ferocity).

The other objective of the Church was an attempt to specifically
limit the way in which feudal war was waged. Also at the Fourth
Lateran Council, a canon was directed against the use of a new
and deadly weapon, the *arbalest* or crossbow, decreeing that it
was "a deadly and God detested" weapon and that those who
used it against "Christians and Catholics" should be
anathema.[16] The immediate impression is that this was an attempt
to "humanize" the weapons of war; but many weapons inflicted
much greater suffering on a combatant than a bolt from a
crossbow. More probably the Church's intent was to restrain the
use of weapons, which could have the effect of destroying the
military monopoly of the knight. Once military commanders
discovered that a disciplined body of lowborn footmen, armed
with an inexpensive weapon, could inflict heavy losses on feudal
cavalry, war would no longer be confined to such a small number
of combatants. If the knight and his code suffered eclipse the effect would be felt by both the Church and the civil population,
which were enjoying a period of relative security unknown since
the days of *pax Romana*. Unfortunately the Church was as unsuccessful in halting the general adoption of the crossbow as it
had been in abolishing tournaments. Yet these instances of specific
restrictions are noteworthy not so much for what they failed to
accomplish but for what they attempted: to perpetuate and at
the same time constrain the knightly code. The condemnation
of the crossbow was not an effort only to ban a weapon but to
limit violence to the professionals while leaving the rest of society undisturbed.

All of these institutions were spontaneous products of Christian society. They were not the results of careful theological or
philosophical doctrines; rather, they arose in response to felt social
needs, and quickly obtained formal sanction from the leadership
of society. It is an example of intuition and moral sensitivity com-

bining with necessity to fill gaps in formal reasoning. However, one should not attribute to these rules, nor to their sponsors, a sophistication they did not possess. For example, it will be recalled that the rules were constantly invoked for "Christians" and "Christian men." Though the official decrees were intended to apply only to Christians, this does not necessarily mean that Jews and Saracens were considered fair game for war's excesses. The *Capitularies* of Charlemagne and various Spanish codes of civil legislation specifically extended protection to these groups. Yet, that this had to be done specifically shows to what extent there was a blindness to the universal applicability of humanitarian principles in the Middle Ages. The best characterization of this might be "moral parochialism." Nowhere is this more evident than in warfare between Christians and Saracens, in which no rules of fair play or mercy were particularly applicable or expected.[17]

This leads to another point. The whole intent of the prescriptions of the Peace of God was to ameliorate suffering for certain classes in private wars. Waging war in an agricultural society, wherein the primary means of exchange was goods in kind, to destroy a man's property was to condemn him and others to hardship or even starvation. When immunity was extended to cattle and draught animals, the intent of the rule was to safeguard the life of the beast's owner and those he might feed and clothe. This undoubtedly accounts for the somewhat disproportionate immunity provided for property. At the same time, since the purpose of private wars was invariably to acquire booty rather than to simply destroy an enemy, it was reasonable to emphasize the immunity of those objects most prized as ends of these wars.

Yet one also perceives that in the minds of those who established the categories of immune classes there was still a considerable ambivalence as to precisely why those classes should be immune. Thus one is reminded again of the parochialism of feudal society. The first immunity decrees applied to ecclesiastics and to the property but not the persons of the poor; only later were all women and other defenseless classes such as merchants and pilgrims included. Later still, serfs and their property were declared immune from attack, at which point the reason is given for the first time that homicide of these Christians is wrong because it is equivalent to shedding the blood of Christ. This observation does not imply that the rule makers' motivations failed to include a humanitarian regard for defenseless life. The progressive inclusion of more and more categories under the protection of immunity represents simply an increasingly explicit awareness of those who both theoretically should and practically could be protected. However, the formulators of these rules were not acting upon a clear-cut set of principles that accorded a fundamental right of immunity to all defenseless persons regardless of religious belief. With all the humanitarian and charitable impulses that actuated the medieval peacemakers, they still did not accept the notion that an "enemy" possessed "rights."

The only persons who really fitted the category of "enemy" in the Middle Ages were non-Christians. According to the Augustinian-Thomistic notion of war, few of the private quarrels that nobles engaged in could have qualified as "just wars," and even less would the serfs, pilgrims, merchants, and ecclesiastics have fitted the category of an "enemy population." They were simply unfortunate, unintended victims. As they were Christians who suffered at the hands of other Christians, it was easy enough to deduce the necessity of sparing them from this violence in Christ's name. In fact, such a notion needed only formal proclamation to receive ready acceptance from Christians of all classes.

A true "enemy," however, such as the Moslem, was looked upon as being unworthy of merciful treatment. Numerous sources detail the unchivalrous conduct of the Crusaders in their relations with the "infidel." A religious war, what today might be called an "ideological" struggle, with its absolute objectives, added to the frustrations that soldiers experienced in intra-Christian warfare, and tended to loosen the restraints of Christian conflict that took so long and so much difficulty to establish. It is true that acts of chivalry and mercy may be found in the histories of the Crusades, although most often credited to the Saracens. But these were exceptions to the general rule, and the probability is that the likes of Richard *Coeur de Lion* felt more restrained by his warrior's code of fair fight than by any commitment to Christian mercy. Acts of chivalry between participating warriors are beside the point, anyway. What is at issue is the attitude of the warrior toward the defenseless, and here the conclusion can only be that to the Crusader the enemy was morally guilty and that vengeful destruction was his due.[18]

This attitude could hardly be otherwise when one recalls the Christian theology of war to this time. Nevertheless, the contribution of the Medieval peace movements to the developing notion of immunity for noncombatants was enormous. Many of the groups of the population that came to be accepted as immune in war were first so designated by the Peace of God, which passed then into the chivalric code, and finally became ingrained in the European consciousness. Though much evolution was still required before a full-blown ethical principle of noncombatant immunity was established, at least the customary acceptance of some such principle was founded. The next important change in Christian just war theory, in the later Middle Ages, was a modification of the Augustinian-Thomistic view of war as a punishment and of the enemy as subjectively guilty. Such a change, when it came, made it possible to apply the principles of Christian mercy to all.

Part III
Modern Synthesis

VII The Innocent Becomes the Noncombatant

If we must fight, why not go against the common enemy, the Turk? But wait. Is not the Turk also a man and a brother?

Erasmus, *The Complaint of Peace*

In the past half century the work of Francisco de Vitoria has enjoyed a limited revival, primarily because of a new appreciation of him as a forerunner of Hugo Grotius in the establishment of international law.[1] A Spanish theologian, a friar in the Order of St. Dominic, and a scholar at the University of Salamanca, Vitoria is an example of an intellectual who never stirred from his study, but whose work was to have a profound effect on later thought. His life (1486-1546) spanned the period of the Spanish discovery and conquest of the New World and much of the Counter-Reformation, an epoch of radical change.

For Vitoria, as for his predecessors, there was no doubt that war, even offensive war, could be just and that under certain conditions it should not trouble the Christian conscience. A vital question for Vitoria, however, was the degree of force that was permissible in a just war. His view is worth quoting at length.

> Here let my first proposition be: in war everything is lawful which the defense of the common weal requires. This is notorious, for the end and aim of war is the defense and preservation of the State. Also, a private person may do this in self-defense, as has been proved. Therefore, much more may a State and a prince . . . .[2] A prince may go even further in a just war and do whatever is necessary in order to obtain peace and security from the enemy . . . . Therefore a belligerent may do everything requisite to obtain peace and security . . . . Therefore it is lawful to employ all appropriate measures against enemies who are plundering and disturbing the tranquility of the State.[3]

On the nature and purpose of just war, Vitoria was a traditionalist. For him, a further proof of the right to wage offensive war was "that even a defensive war could not be waged satisfactorily, were not vengeance taken on enemies who have done or tried to do a wrong. For they would not be emboldened to make a second attack, if the fear of retribution did not keep them from wrong-doing."[4]

The immediate impression one receives from these and similar statements is that Vitoria's views on just war follow the rigid Augustinian-Thomistic tradition without variation: The primary purpose of just war is vengeance for moral wrongdoing, and a just cause inherently involves the establishment of the enemy's subjective guilt. Though this position has been ascribed to Vitoria by some commentators,[5] it is an erroneous interpretation. Perhaps the most balanced consideration of this point is by Robert Regout, who has correctly observed that a crucial difference between Vitoria and most medieval authors was his eventual insistence that a concrete or objective violation of a right was not necessarily coupled with subjective, moral guilt.[6] Basing his conclusions on the whole range of Vitoria's writings, especially the very important texts in Vitoria's commentary on St. Thomas's *Summa,* Regout argues convincingly that Vitoria's is a truly original view of just war. This evolution of perspective was to prove vital because it led to a theory of just war that was less severe, less absolute, and more realistic than the stricter medieval position.[7] But here it is best to allow Vitoria to speak for himself.

In his commentary on St. Thomas's *Summa theologica,* Vitoria takes up the moral problems pertaining to war. This work is no simple reiteration of Thomas's thought; rather, it is a thoroughly contemporary, lucidly phrased sixteenth century exposition. Vitoria's comments in this context demonstrate the degree to which he goes beyond his master in applying accepted principles to living fact. The most important aspect of his discussion here is on the proper way of waging the just war. His statement of a fourth condition, the *debitus modus* or proper procedure, added to the inherited Scholastic formulation of proper preconditions. It is because of this addition that the matured Christian theory of just war was to stress *jus in bello.*

In article 1 of question 40, he raises the question whether it is permissible to slay in warfare. He replies in predictable fashion "that if this act is necessary to victory, it is permissible, just as it is permissible to slay individuals who disturb the state."[8] But, he says, a question arises in this connection:

> Let us suppose that the Spanish have been victorious, they are no longer fearful of danger; but their enemies are fleeing: is it permissible to pursue the latter and slay them assuming, as I have suggested, that their death is no longer necessary to the victory [of the Spanish]?[9]

Vitoria answers that it is entirely permissible to slay them because a king possesses power not only to recover his property but also to chastize those who have injured him and his people. If it were not so, there would be no deterrent to wrongdoing. But, "I hold that it would not be permissible to slay all of the enemy; on the contrary, moderation should be observed"[10] because all the enemy are not responsible.

> Thirdly I hold that it is not permissible to slay any of the enemy, after victory has been won, in cases in which they were fighting licitly, provided that there is no longer any danger threatened from them.[11]

Next, and perhaps most important, Vitoria deals specifically with the innocent in time of war. "Doubt arises as to whether innocent children may be slain in this war."[12] Vitoria answers this rhetorical doubt negatively.

> The reason for this restriction is clear; for these persons are innocent, neither is it needful to the attainment of victory that they should be slain. It would be heretical to say that it is licit to kill them. . . . Accordingly, the innocent may not be slain by [primary] intent, when it is possible to distinguish them from the guilty.[13]

Not quoted here but included in this passage are Vitoria's careful conditions outlining under what circumstances the innocent may be licitly slain, for example, if their death results in the course of a siege of a fortified city. Further, he stresses that all persons able to bear arms should be generally considered not innocent.

Vitoria introduces two thoroughly innovative notions. First, he prohibits any slaughter of the innocent by "primary intent," thereby employing for the first time in any discussion of *jus in bello* the Thomistic principle of "double effect."[14] Second, he makes clear that guilt or innocence is a material, objective fact, determined by the bearing or nonbearing of arms. In short, the only legitimate military target among an enemy population are those who are obviously dangerous.[15] He reinforces these statements in another work entitled *De jure belli.*[16]

> The basis of a just war is a wrong done, as has been shown above. But wrong is not done by an innocent person. Therefore war may not be employed against him. . . . Thirdly, it is not lawful within a State to punish the innocent for the wrongdoing of the guilty. Therefore this is not lawful among enemies.[17]

Vitoria's following statement must also be quoted at length, because in it he not only expands on his initial principles but explicitly designates those categories of people who must be presumed innocent. Here, as in a previous statement, the innocent among the Turks are included.

> Here it follows that even in war with the Turks it is not allowable to kill children. This is clear, because they are innocent. Aye, and the same holds with regard to the women of unbelievers. This is clear, because so far as the war is concerned, they are presumed innocent; but it does not hold in the case of any individual woman who is certainly guilty. Aye, and this same pronouncement must be made among Christians with regard to harmless agricultural folk, and also with regard to the rest of the peaceable civilian population, for all these are presumed innocent until the contrary is shown. On this principle it follows that it is not lawful to slay either foreigners or guests who are sojourning among the enemy, for they are presumed innocent, and in truth they are not enemies. The same principle applies to clerics and members of a religious order, for they in war are presumed innocent unless the contrary be shown, as when they engage in actual fighting.[18]

But what of the practical situation in which the innocent are so intermingled with the guilty that to distinguish them is difficult if not impossible?

Sometimes it is right, in virtue of collateral circumstances to slay the innocent even knowingly, as when a fortress or city is stormed in a just war, although it is known that there are a number of innocent people in it and although cannon and other engines of war cannot be discharged or fire applied to buildings without destroying innocent together with guilty. The proof is that war could not otherwise be waged against even the guilty and the justice of belligerents would be balked. In the same way, conversely, if a town be wrongfully besieged and rightfully defended, it is lawful to fire cannon shot and other missiles on the besiegers and into the hostile camp, even though we assume that there are some children and innocent people there.[19]

Vitoria goes on to warn that care must be taken so that evils greater than the good that is achieved do not result. If there are in a besieged city so few guilty that the issue of the war is not at stake, then it would not be lawful to kill many innocent persons merely to punish the few guilty. "In sum, it is never right to slay the guiltless, even as an indirect and unintended result (much less directly and intentionally), except when there is no other means of carrying on the operations of a just war. . . ."[20]

With these various applications of the basic principle that it is never licit to intentionally slay the innocent, Vitoria raises another doubt. He asks whether guiltless persons may be killed because in the future they may become enemies—for example, the children of Saracens, who no doubt will fight Christians when they grow up. Vitoria answers that though this practice may be defended, he can see no justification for it because "it is intolerable that any one should be killed for a future fault."[21] However, not only should children be spared[22] but also soldiers, actual combatants, when they are no longer dangerous. "Hence it follows that, whether victory has already been won or the war is still in progress, if the innocence of any soldier is evident and the soldiers can let him go free, they are bound to do so."[23] This view conformed to a later expression on the killing of hostages. On the question of killing hostages when the enemy has broken faith, Vitoria answers that

If the hostages are in other respects among the guilty, as for instance, because they have borne arms, they may rightfully be killed in that case; if, however, they are innocent as for instance, if they be children or women or other innocent folk, it is obvious from what has been said above that they cannot be killed.[24]

Clearly, then, for Vitoria, the innocent among the enemy should be immune from slaughter. But what of the guilty? May they be slain indiscriminately when they have surrendered? As to soldiers who have surrendered, since as combatants they may be presumed guilty, Vitoria says that "speaking absolutely, there is nothing to prevent the killing of those who have surrendered or been captured in a just war so long as abstract equity is observed."[25] But whereas he can think of no absolute principle that would be violated by such a procedure, he nevertheless qualifies this statement radically, and in so doing gives as his justification for the qualification the accepted rules and customs among people.

Many of the rules of war have, however, been fashioned by the law of nations, and it seems to be received in the use and custom of war that captives, after victory has been won (unless perchance they have been routed) and all danger is over, are not to be killed and the law of nations must be respected, as is the wont among good people.[26]

Though numerous other texts could be cited as examples of Vitoria's views, they would be largely repetitious. However, it is necessary to quote from the last pages of *De jure belli,* where Vitoria sums up in three brief canons or "rules of warfare" all that he has said previously. Canons 2 and 3 pertain directly to the conduct of war and may be taken as his final opinion on the matter. Canon 2 states:

When war for a just cause has broken out, it must not be waged so as to ruin the people against whom it is directed, but only so as to obtain one's rights and the defense of one's country and in order that from the war peace and security may in time result.[27]

This attitude of restraint, moderation, and limitation in the waging of war should be carried over when victory has been won and peace restored. Canon 3 states in part:

When victory has been won and the war is over, the victory should be utilized with moderation and Christian humility, and the victor ought to deem that he is sitting as judge between two States . . . and this, so far as possible, should involve the offending State in the least degree of calamity and misfortune, the offending individuals being chastised within lawful limits; and an especial reason for this is that in general among Christians all the fault is to be laid at the door of their princes, for subjects when fighting for their princes act in good faith.[28]

Nowhere is Vitoria's humanitarianism more evident than in these passages.

It is obvious that Vitoria held forceful opinions on the unlawfulness of slaying the innocent and, starting from this premise, applied the principle to particular cases. But on what authority or line of reasoning did his initial premise depend? Vitoria leaves no doubt about his philosophical presuppositions. After quoting Augustine and Thomas Aquinas on the just cause of war, he states unequivocally, "Hence it is clear that we may not turn our sword against those who do us no harm, *the killing of the innocent being forbidden by natural law.*"[29] Here he states explicitly what was only implied by followers of St. Thomas, such as Antoninus of Florence. Since Thomas's statement on the nature and division of law, his followers had progressively applied his analysis to an increasing range of subjects. Vitoria supplies not only an avowal that natural law forbids the direct killing of the innocent but also a careful definition of who these innocent are and why they should be presumed innocent.

Vitoria's enumeration of the groups in the population that should be considered immune because of their innocence is traditional, with some very notable exceptions. Besides women and children, and "among Christians," harmless agricultural folk, traveling foreigners, clerics, and religious, Vitoria includes the women and children of the Saracens, and enemy soldiers no longer capable of causing damage.[30] Though Vitoria relies on the customary designation of immune classes originated by the Peace of God, his specific inclusion of infidel women and children in the category of the immune and his contention that there are innocent among the enemy soldiery who must be spared when possible mark a sophistication of thought his predecessors did not possess.

As to why these classes should be considered innocent until the contrary has been proven, Vitoria makes clear his grounds. In numerous instances, but especially in the one cited above, Vitoria calls upon the law of customary relations among nations. It will be recalled that when Vitoria discussed the legitimate fate of captured soldiers he urged that they be spared because such was the custom.[31] Again he refers to the law of nations in discussing the enslavement of Christians: "But inasmuch as, by the law of nations, it is a received rule of Christendom that Christians do not become slaves in right of war, this enslaving is not lawful in a war between Christians."[32]

Though the humanitarian sparing of "guilty" enemy soldiers and the complex problem of enslavement (which Vitoria did allow when the enemy were Saracens)[33] do not pertain specifically to the question of innocent immunity, Vitoria's reliance on the law of nations is tantamount to an indirect appeal to natural law, and in turn hints of the connection between the law of nations and the specification of particular classes as immune. This is not the place to explore Vitoria's conception of the relationship between the law of nations and the natural law. Suffice it to say that the relationship is direct and intimate. However, the following comment is an excellent appraisal of this relationship in Vitoria's thought.

> The constraining force of the law of nations is intimately connected with the natural law. For as necessity was the basis for the latter's compulsive power so the obligation of the law of nations is based on its relative or hypothetical necessity for the observance of the natural law, from which it arises as a rational deduction.[34]

The customary practices that form the substance of the law of nations are therefore indirectly or immediately referable to the natural law. Whereas natural law evidently, as a rational deduction, strictly forbids the direct slaying of the innocent, the customary rules of the law of nations determine concrete rules of action, such as proscribing the enslaving of Christians and allowing the enslaving of Saracens.

An important conclusion about the innocent in war can be drawn from Vitoria's appeal to the law of nations. Whereas natural law simply forbids that the innocent may ever be killed directly, the law of nations can serve as an adequate, precise, and concrete guide to determine who should be presumed innocent in wartime. Even if practice and custom did not include women and children in the immune category, their status as innocents would be self-evident. But the other classes who should also be included in this immunity may be less evident. However, through the development of custom certain classes of the population had been progressively treated as innocent. As custom and reason developed, the necessity for immunizing these classes became more and more evident and consequently more necessary. The gradual inclusion of new classes in the immune category, in Vitoria's mind, depended upon an experiential determination in differing contexts as to whether these individuals or classes are in fact innocent. When custom established such a specific determination, this establishment should be considered part of the law of nations, and as such sufficiently obligatory that it ought not to be arbitrarily abrogated.

Custom among Christians had long immunized farmers, laborers, pilgrims, and religious. But custom itself rested upon practical criteria, which may be summarized as follows: These people could be presumed innocent because they did not bear arms; they did not actively participate or engage in the unjust aggression; as innocents, they should be immune from slaughter until their guilt was proven by an unjust act. Therefore, their guilt or innocence, and hence their status as legitimate objects of attack or as immune from direct attack, should be contingent upon an objective, material fact: their participation or nonparticipation in unjust activity.

The great significance of Vitoria's general views on the just causes and the purpose of just war is that, with less stress on the enemy's subjective *culpa* or guilt and more emphasis on the enemy's objective unjust act, the "enemy" can be concretely specified as those who are actually combatants. No longer need there be a vague identification of the enemy as a mass of wrong-willed individuals whose subjective guilt must be certified or supposed. According to such a criterion a determination of the innocent is almost impossible. This does not mean that for Vitoria combatants were not subjectively guilty: they were, but by the same token noncombatants were innocent in the traditional, subjective moral sense. The point is that at last a suitable criterion, still based upon presumably absolute moral principles, was stated, one that provided a clear and certain guide for right action. The resultant principle of noncombatant immunity was therefore a norm derived in part from deductive moral reasoning but dependent for its clear practical application upon accepted custom.

Vitoria established a real existence for an abstract moral concept: "innocence" was now a concrete reality. The spirit of innocence could have real form as "the uninvolved." His work demanded of his audience a confrontation of theory with practice, compelling a union of the two. Philosophy and dogmatic theology must unite, he seemed to say, in order to supplement and be supplemented by the custom of peoples, a custom he viewed as having an intuition of its own. With Vitoria the civilian was no longer an abstract "innocent"; he had become an actual person who deserved immunity because he was not responsible in any personal way for the conduct of war. Whether Turk or Christian, his immune status should be guaranteed because he was innocent: the natural law so proclaimed, and the law of nations sanctioned it.

Yet, a generation after Vitoria's death in 1546, the Christian Knights of St. John, besieged by the Turks on Malta, were feeding their cannon with the heads of slaughtered prisoners in retaliation for a similarly barbarous act on the part of their attackers.[35] But the impassioned vision of Erasmus was not so Utopian as it might have seemed, and the careful argumentation of Vitoria was not in vain. A new era was dawning, one so replete with internecine cruelty among Christians that thoughtful men were driven by their own revulsion of it to seek a new and more humane guide to war's conduct. Not surprisingly, they looked back with gratitude to the foundation that had been laid by Francisco de Vitoria.

VIII

The Emergence of the Civilian

> It is the bidding of mercy, if not of justice, that, except for reasons that are weighty and will affect the safety of many, no action should be attempted whereby innocent persons may be threatened with destruction.
>
> Hugo Grotius, *De jure belli ac pacis libri tres*

It is conventional wisdom that a scientific principle, regardless of its objective validitiy, must have a hospitable environment before its truth will be perceived. The time must be right. So it is with norms of social behavior, which emerge from the stresses of human necessity. The combination of internal logic and external events ordains their acceptance. For the notion of civilian immunity, the confluence of events that occurred in the sixteenth and seventeenth centuries provided the habitat in which the concept could assume practical relevance. The events were varied and it is futile to attempt to discriminate degrees of causal importance in the shaping of the final effect. Nevertheless, historical hindsight does indicate the extraordinary impact that the new science, philosophy, economics, and politics of this period were to have on the maturation of civilian immunity.

The appearance of sovereign nation-states with accompanying and consequent rebellions and wars, the success of the Protestant Reformation and the resultant secularization of many institutions previously given religious meaning, the wealth of a New World, and the economic disruption of the old order that ensued—these and many other events brought forth a society desparately in need of a new transnational legal order. The effort to found such an order was one of the major preoccupations of some of Europe's finest minds in the seventeenth and eighteenth centuries. The cornerstone of modern international law

was laid by these writers, most of them secular jurists. The giant
among them was Hugo Grotius.

His was the era of the secularization of just war theory. The
notion that the noninvolved, nonresponsible nonwarrior should
be afforded respect and protection in time of war stepped out
of the confines of theological *tractatae,* canonical decrees and
princely declarations to stand as a public rule, binding civilized
nations who were engaged in otherwise uncivil conduct. If war
seemed inevitable and its justice questionable, at least some
measure of humanity could be retained by denying the warring
parties a license to kill the defenseless. But before Grotius made
his statement in *De jure belli ac pacis* and before the secular men
of law and letters assumed the burden laid down by the
theologians, there was a transitional period during which dying
Scholasticism helped give life to the new secular ideal.

Foremost among the theological successors of Vitoria was the
Spanish Jesuit, Francisco Suarez (1548–1617), an antagonist of
the Protestant Reformation. Suarez is rightly considered the last
of the Scholastics, with his vast works constituting a final statement of Medieval-Rennaisance philosophy and theology. No one
better summarized the tradition to which he was heir, and no
one better presaged the replacement of that tradition.

In his work on the three theological virtues of faith, hope, and
charity, Suarez takes up the problem of just war.[1] To the question of who is liable to punishment in a just war, he replies:

> In answering this question we must note that some of these per-
> sons (the enemy) are said to be guilty, and others innocent. It is
> implicit in natural law that the innocent include children, women,
> and all unable to bear arms; by the *jus gentium,* ambassadors,
> and among Christians, by positive (canon) law (Decretals, Bk.
> I, tit. XXXIV, chap. ii), religious persons, priests & c . . . . All
> other persons are considered guilty; for human judgment looks
> upon those able to take up arms as having actually done so.[2]

Suarez clearly indicates that the category of "innocence" includes
individuals who might or might not be "innocent" in the subjective moral sense. Three sources combine to establish the persons
in this category as innocents: natural law, *jus gentium* (which

would include custom and written law), and canon law. Only in the first instance can it be assumed that Suarez advocates immunity for women and children because of a presumed subjective innocence. In the other two instances, persons are innocent because of objective, material fact. For Suarez, the innocent category, that group for whom immunity should be presumed as a right, is composed of those whom deductive moral reasoning and customary law and usage had together provided protection from attack. What single feature or characteristic is shared by all these classes of people, that requires their protection as innocents? Suarez explicitly says that, aside from those enumerated, all others in a state are said to be guilty, and these are guilty because they are able to bear arms. Their ability to engage in an objective act of injustice would justify the liability of "all other persons" to attack in a just war, except that the very fact of their not engaging in war, despite having the capacity to do so, gives prima facie evidence of their innocence:

> But one may ask, who actually are the innocent, with respect to this issue? My reply is that they include not only the persons enumerated above, but also those who are able to bear arms, if it is evident that, in other respects, they have not shared in the crime nor in the unjust war; for the natural law demands that, generally speaking, no one who is actually known to be free from guilt, shall be slain.[3]

Hence, Suarez narrows down what had been a rather sweeping injuction that all who had the "ability" to bear arms were guilty; more important, however, he confirms the view that it is the perpetration of a crime, a *delict,* that makes one a legitimate target of attack. These statements of Suarez support the conclusion that: "This distinction between the innocent and the guilty is essentially a distinction between combatants and noncombatants."[4]

As to the absoluteness of this immunity, Suarez's position is perfectly consistent with the accepted Scholastic view. "I hold that innocent persons as such may in nowise be slain, even if the punishment inflicted upon their state would, otherwise, be deemed inadequate; but incidentally they may be slain, when such an act is necessary in order to secure victory."[5] The reason for this "is that the slaying of innocent persons is intrinsically evil."[6] However, the innocent may be killed incidentally when such is a necessary means to attain victory ("as in the burning of cities and the destruction of fortresses"):[7]

> In such a case, the death of the innocent is not sought for its own sake, but is an incidental consequence; hence, it is considered not as voluntarily inflicted but simply as allowed by one who is making use of his right in a time of necessity.[8]

Without elaborating the nuances of Suarez's thought, it is clear that in some respects he offered refinements of his predecessors's presentations on the moral limits of war's conduct. Suarez built upon the Vitorian synthesis of the principle of noncombatant immunity, adding nothing new to it. However, his treatment of the principle is particularly clear and concise while including all the necessary elements: immunity of the innocent is based on the moral law, and the status of innocence depends upon nonparticipation in the active prosecution of injustice. The final Scholastic statement had been made; the writings of Suarez mark the end of Scholastic thought on the subject of just war and its proper conduct. It is almost as though the moralists and theologians left the field by common consent, for nothing of substance is heard from them again until the resurrection of just war theorizing after World War II.

This abdication of concern for the ethical dimensions of human conflict control is difficult to explain, coming as it does so abruptly and after so many centuries of intense and fruitful speculation. Perhaps it was due to an exhaustion of original insight, a confidence that the last word had been spoken on the subject, an accommodation to nationalist interest, and/or other factors. Whatever the reasons, one unfortunate result was that the newly emerging positive international law did not have the support of a continuing, parallel body of moral theorizing about the justice of war's conduct. Without such a support, the new law came to depend exclusively on a functional and pragmatic base, and its appeal to an increasingly sceptical audience was necessarily one-dimensional.[9] It can be argued that changed circumstances in post-Reformation Europe greatly reduced the authority and influence of Catholic writers. Their motives and objectivity would naturally be doubted by a new generation of Protestant rulers who had recently shed the yoke of Roman dogmatism. Yet Protestant ethical theoreticians were as unconcerned as their Catholic antagonists with the moral implications of warfare in this new age. Instead, during the sixteenth and seventeenth centuries, it was the professional lawyers and soldiers who were increasingly concerned with limiting the destructiveness of war. Representative of the latter group was Balthasar Ayala (1548-1584), a Spanish nobleman who served Phillip II as Auditor General in the Netherlands. Ayala's *On the Law and Duties of War*[10] exemplifies the transition from theoretical and religious preoccupations to practical and secular concerns. He relies heavily on ancient secular writers and on such contemporaries as Jean Bodin to a far greater extent than had his Scholastic predecessors, and he deals, as they had not, with the consequences of unjust war.

Ayala's primary concern is with military discipline and with appropriate tactics to keep the peace after a war is won. His appeal is to the military commander, not the soldier in the ranks, and hence he says little about the broader ethical questions of humane conduct during conflict. This is due not to his disagreement with or ignorance of the established rules of fair conduct but rather, as he clearly implies, because he takes them for granted and sees no reason to be repetitious. He quotes an ancient source with approval, the sparing of captured youths by Camillus, and then observes:

> Of course, severity towards women and the young was always reckoned very disgraceful, their very sex and age exempting them from the hazards of battle and the rage of the conqueror . . . . The canons indeed contain an injunction that the following be spared: clergy, monks, converts, foreigners, merchants, and country folk.[11]

Though some opinion maintains that these immunities have been "abrogated by contrary usage,"[12] Ayala contends that this is probably not so, as far as nonfighting clergy is concerned. What is important about Ayala's oblique references to innocent immunity is that he, as a military advisor, indicates full awareness of accepted custom in this matter and obviously approves of it. The significance is that, as a soldier, he is addressing his military peers toward an end that apparently was not contested but rather was taken for granted: Under all circumstances, the innocent (well-defined as noncombatants of various classes) should be mercifully treated, unless demands of military necessity make this impossible.[13] This position is echoed by another nonreligious predecessor of Grotius and a near contemporary of Suarez, Alberico Gentili.[14] Lapses in military discipline continued to occur in this period, but more and more these breaches were considered exceptional. The public practice of Europe was catching up with its theory. Then, as if to immediately give the lie to this evolution, the Thirty Years' War erupted in 1618.

There is no need to dwell at length on the barbarity of the thirty years of bloodshed that engulfed Europe. The senseless waste of human beings and material resources was perhaps unmatched until this century. All the synonyms for evil are exhausted in describing this conflict, during which it is said, "Cannibalism grew so rife that bodies were torn from the gallows by hunger-maddened folk, and thoughout the Rhineland the very graveyards were guarded because of the traffic in human flesh."[15] One historian has estimated that more than 7,500,000 persons died in Germany alone, one-third of its entire population.[16] With bitter irony one is reminded of Tertullian's defense of the early Christian community, "See these Christians, how they love one another," for the times appeared totally devoid of love among Christians.

Ridicule of the expressed religious motivations of those years of struggle is appropriate since the tragedy was really played out for dynastic reasons. At issue was the course and survival of the Holy Roman Empire, the Low Countries' independence from Spanish hegemony, and Swedish superiority of arms. Princely venality governed political policy. The common practice of employing mercenaries, whose payment was the loot they could extract from the countryside and its inhabitants, is itself an indicator of what the noncombatants' plight must have been.[17]

Into this malestrom a voice of reason intruded itself to proclaim,

There is a common law among nations, which is valid alike for
war and in war . . . . Throughout the Christian world I observed
a lack of restraint in relation to war, such as even barbarous races
should be ashamed of: I observed that men rush to arms for slight
causes, or no cause at all, and that when arms have once been
taken up there is no longer any respect for law, divine or human;
it is as if, in accordance with a general decree, frenzy had openly
been let loose for the committing of all crime.[18]

That Hugo Grotius was the father of modern international law
need hardly be noted here, although he himself acknowledged
his debt to his predecessors, especially Vitoria. He would have
been the first to decline the title, but his work was the most influential source for modern, positive international law. What was
lacking in originality was more than compensated for by the clari-
ty and comprehensiveness of his presentation.

With no equivocation, he entitles chapter 11 of his great work
De jure belli ac pacis libri tres, published in 1625, "Moderation
with Respect to the Right of Killing in a Lawful War."[19] Citing
innumerable sources from a vast range of historical and
philosophic literature, Grotius builds his case that "One must take
care, so far as is possible, to prevent the death of innocent persons, even by accident," because "it is the bidding of mercy, if
not of justice, that except for reasons that are weighty and will
affect the safety of many, no action should be attempted whereby
innocent persons may be threatened with destruction."[20]

After indicating the obligation to safeguard the innocent in time
of war, Grotius insists that children should always be spared,
as should women, "unless they have been guilty of an extremely
serious offense; and old men."[21] Women should enjoy absolute
immunity from attack if they commit no crime "unless they take
the place of men."[22] The inference here was that they would forfeit
their innocent status if they took up arms like men. Unless otherwise proved by their actions, women should be granted the benefit
of doubt and assumed to be innocent. So, too, those in certain
occupations such as religious, men of letters, farmers, and
merchants.[23]

Of special note is why Grotius classifies these persons as immune from attack. He says they are so because "nature does not sanction retaliation except against those who have done wrong. It is not sufficient that by a sort of fiction the enemy may be conceived as forming a single body."[24] With this statement, the humanization of war, if that is not a contradiction in terms, took a giant stride forward.

Many of Grotius's predecessors had stated or implied the same concept, that though "enemy" was a collective term, distinction of responsibility among the enemy populations was necessary. But however fine the logic and humane the outlook, even the most sophisticated of his predecessors (such as Vitoria) had difficulty escaping from what might be called the "ideological taint" or crusade mentality that always justified some qualification. The ancient notion of collective guilt, so starkly enunciated by Augustine many centuries before, had remained an implicit, if increasingly underplayed, assumption. Hence, even sensitive consciences could reconcile the savagery of the Thirty Years' War in the name of God, or suspend the rules if the foe was non-Christian. What Grotius was insisting upon was the obvious reality that, though states go to war, it is individuals who wage them. In the next century another visionary, Jean Jacques Rousseau, echoed the spirit of the great Dutch jurist when he observed,

> War is therefore not a concern between man and man but between State and State, in which individuals are only enemies accidentally, not as men, or as citizens, but as soldiers; not as members of a country but as its defenders. In fine, States can only have other States, and not men, for enemies, because there can be no true relation between things of different natures.[25]

No doubt an important element in Grotius's emphasis was his own obsession with toleration. All his life his major interest and hope was for a reconciliation of fractured Christianity. A devout Protestant, he just as devoutly urged a reunification of Christendom and an end to the fratricidal slaughter that Europe was experiencing.

More than merely a charitable temperament determined Grotius's conclusions.[26] The most important motive was philosophical, the oftnoted intellectual stepchild of the Protestant Reformation: the secularization of medieval natural law. Much has been written about the sources and ramifications of this philosophic turnabout; a brief summary of the concepts involved is necessary to fully appreciate its effect on Grotius and on the philosophers and jurists who succeeded him.[27]

The pre-Reformation Christian mind considered "nature" and "grace" as separate phenomena. The central theme of Christian theology was the way in which nature was perfected by grace, an occurrence made possible only by the incarnation of God in the person of Jesus. Hence, in the strictest sense, only the Christian could rise above or perfect his nature, since only to him, through baptism and belief, was grace available. For Catholic writers, the realm of justice in ethical thought was related to nature, whereas the realm of charity or mercy derived from Christian virtue was based upon grace. Suarez is the nearest writer to Grotius who follows this tradition and who discusses just war and its conduct, appropriately enough, in his discourse on the virtue of charity. The burden of this position is obvious in the inability of these thinkers to completely put aside a Christian/non-Christian distinction when considering the necessity to spare the innocent among the enemy. Though the later Scholastics had escaped the harshness of the original Augustinian view, and Vitoria had shown the way in extending immunity to non-Christian as well as Christian enemies, the innocent among the latter deserved to be spared for a different reason than the former: civilian Christians should be spared because as Christians they deserved consideration founded not in nature alone but in moral dicta rooted in a yet higher morality, a nature perfected by grace; non-Christian civilians were deserving of immunity as well but because a natural conventional justice required it. The result is rather Orwellian: all men are equal, but some are more equal than others.

One conclusion might be that such a distinction is really too arcane to matter, but this is to miss the importance of the progressive broadening of the understanding of what it means to be human, a central theme in this study. It is only because of this broadening of definition that the present norm of civilian immunity can be supported. The philosophers of the classic age of Greece held that all non-Greeks were barbarians. Christianity challenged this notion and declared that all men were brothers, especially if they accepted a common belief. Now, in the seventeenth century and the age of Grotius, the number of those considered beyond the pale was reduced further, extending theoretically by a quantum leap the human beings who deserved to be treated equally, as uninvolved, innocent nonvictims during war.

Grotius himself is not solely responsible for this change; Suarez had hinted at it. What Grotius aimed for in his emphasis on "moderation" was a view of human nature that was more naturalistic, less dependent on particular religious belief, and hence more potentially extensive to a greater number of persons. The concept of nature did not so much replace grace as it blended with and subsumed it, thereby extending the dimensions of both. It remained to later jurists and philosophers to elaborate this theme, but the theoretical base for that elaboration was established by Grotius. The last sentence in Rousseau's earlier cited observation can only be fully appreciated in the context of this new view of nature, and of human nature, which supports its own universally applicable morality. Grotius affirmed that there existed a common right, worthy of claim by all persons simply because they are human. Whatever the other consequences of secularized natural-law thinking were, an undeniable benefit was afforded to the civilian of all nations regardless of his beliefs.

IX   The Maturity of an Illusion

In peace, the progress of knowledge and industry is accelerated by the emulation of so many active rivals: in war, the European forces are exercised by temperate and undecisive contests.

Edward Gibbon, *The History of the Decline and Fall of the Roman Empire*

Democracy made all men equal in theory, but it was conscription which did so in fact . . . the musket made the infantryman, and the infantryman made the democrat.

Major General J.F.C. Fuller, *The Conduct of War, 1789-1961*

The Thirty Years' War was finally ended in 1648 with the Peace of Westphalia, and a battered and bloody Europe faced the task of restoring some modicum of order and humane existence. The degree to which this effort was successful is, in retrospect, remarkable. Europe was to enjoy for more than two centuries a period that, if not entirely peaceful, was at least marked by a sophistication of treatment toward the noncombatant that had rarely if ever been evidenced. Even the dynastic upheaval of the Napoleonic Era could not disrupt the steady progress made in shielding the civilian from the worst ravages of warfare. The eighteenth and nineteenth centuries witnessed the high-water mark of noncombatant immunity. It seems fitting that the developments during these centuries should be ratified precisely at the end of the nineteenth century and the beginning of the twentieth with the Hague Conventions of 1899 and 1907. For the civilian there was never a better time.

A review of this period, from the last decades of the seventeenth century to the turn of the twentieth, leaves the impression that certain vague but real forces were in conjunction: ideas and practice combined, intuition and policy conformed, soldiers and civilians could be distinguished, and the distinction was largely respected by both parties. As later experience was to prove, however, the conjunction of these forces, though fortuitous, was accidental; for the status achieved by the civilian to the end of the nineteenth century was a gratuitous achievement, a structure built upon an artificial foundation, which required only a slight maladjustment of its composite elements to bring about its collapse. Neither the advance of civilian immunity through the next two centuries nor its retreat in the twentieth could have been imagined by the framers of the Peace of Westphalia. The Peace brought together all the major European powers, excluding only Poland and England. It was achieved by the first modern European congress and possibly deserves recognition as the formal genesis of modern, positive international law.[1]

The Peace fundamentally realigned the power structure of Europe. The Holy Roman Empire was fatally weakened by the separation from it of the Netherlands, Switzerland, and Alsace, and by the recognition of more than three hundred of its territories as virtually sovereign states. The result of this was to forestall the emergence of Germany as a major European power for another two hundred years. Spain lost its claim to the Netherlands and Portugal, and the Catholic Church's political importance was reduced with the granting of international recognition to Protestant states. France emerged as the predominant power on the Continent, while England, untouched by the Thirty Years' War, moved to balance her. Parallel with a sharper definition of European state sovereignty and balance was an intellectual climate of confidence in man's ability to solve any problem by means of reason. The Enlightenment was dawning, and with it a renewed interest in peace as a policy and pity as a practice.

The carnage, hypocrisy, and stupidity of the previous century's conflicts were still fresh in the minds of eighteenth century writers, as the acerbic pens of Voltaire and Jonathan Swift amply testify. In *Candide* and *Gulliver's Travels*, respectively, war is ridiculed as an enterprise unworthy of one who claims to be rational. Gulliver's description to the Houyhnhnms of why and how European princes make war is an unmatched satirical indictment of the pretentions and cruelties of war.[2] In a more straightforward condemnation, another writer, Eymeric Cruce, concluded,

> Why should I, a Frenchman, wish harm to an Englishman, a Spaniard, or a Hindu? I cannot wish it when I consider that they are men like me, that I am subject like them to error and sin and that all nations are bound together by a natural and consequently indestructable tie which insures that a man cannot consider another a stranger.[3]

In addition to negative critiques of Europe's past martial history, the Enlightenment spawned a number of peace proposals. Two of the better known are Immanuel Kant's *Perpetual Peace* and Rousseau's *Judgement sur la paix perpetuelle*. The former argued for universal peace in the name of reason and enlightened self-interest, while the latter urged a federation achieved by force, a distinct echo of his conclusion in *Du contrat social* in which a misled minority would be "forced to be free."[4]

If the intellectual climate of eighteenth century Europe reflected an increased pacifism and support of noncombatant protection, the warfare of the period tended in the same direction. War became limited, not in its incidence but in its scope, duration, and effects on the civilian population. Many reasons have been offered as causes of this phenomenon including ideological, political, social, and technological factors, and no doubt all of them merit consideration. For example, a rigid and mutually suspicious religious division among Christians was greatly reduced. Basking in the confident glow of deistic rationalism, monarchs, generals, philosophers, and scientists were not overly concerned with religion. The Crusade mentality had been largely abandoned, replaced by a faith in science, loyalty to the state, and a near Panglossian confidence that if the world was not yet the best of all possible worlds, it would soon become so.

In this age of enlightened despotism, political stability in Europe had also been achieved. Succession and suzerainty questions had been largely resolved and sovereigns settled down to the task of ordering their own affairs. With political authority thus identified and centralized, the balance of power among states could proceed like a game of chess; kings and queens could deploy their knights and pawns in a predictable and guarded manner.

The effect on warfare of these and other factors was striking. Since threat from the outside was minimized, there was little if any need to arm a citizen soldiery. With sufficient unemployed and unskilled among the lower classes, few nations lacked available manpower to fire their muskets and cannons when the need arose. If some did, there were always foreign mercenaries eager to earn wages and unconcerned with a cause; but these were different mercenaries from their predecessors. They were better paid, better equipped and, most important, better controlled. No longer were they rewarded by booty. Instead a certain renascence of chivalry occurred in the eighteenth century, based on a quaint inversion of the "Golden Rule," which may be paraphrased, "Do not allow your mercenaries to do unto me, lest I allow mine to do unto you." European politics and warfare had indeed come to resemble a massive human chess game.

Mercenaries had to be paid to retain their loyalty. They represented an expensive investment, not to be squandered lightly. Into this eighteenth century play of the balance of power was introduced a ballet interlude in the sense that warfare became, as it had been in the Renaissance, a matter of tactic and maneuver, a stylized dance in which position and honorable surrender were more important than pyrrhic victories. Yet this was also the era of massed formations, drawn up in battle lines facing each other at close range with weapons far more deadly than those with which, at the same range, Greeks and Persians had confronted each other two thousand years before.

In the War of the Austrian Succession, which began in 1741, many of the old European jealousies surfaced. A classic battle was fought at Fontenoy in 1744. Two slightly differing commentaries on the opening of the battle are worth noting.

> When they drew within sixty paces of the French line, Lord Charles Hay stepped out of the allied formation, swept off his hat and drank a toast from his pocket flask. He called for a cheer, which his men gave lustily. The French officers, not to be outdone in international courtesies, returned his salute and ordered

a cheer from their ranks. There followed a taut moment when the opponents stared into the muzzles of muskets at the ready; then just before the volley an English voice was heared in mock prayer, "For what we are about to receive, may the Lord make us truly thankful."[5]

Another version of this incident claims that

When the head of the English column was twenty paces from the French line, the officers of the other side saluted, and Lord Hay, the captain of the Guards, called out: "Tell your men to fire!" But, "No, Sir, you have the honor," replied the Count d'Auteroche. The first volley mowed down the French.[6]

It is probable that such chivalry on the part of their commanders was not appreciated by the men in the ranks. But even if these stories are apocryphal, they do convey the drawing-room politeness that commanders at this time carried into battle. For the noncombatant there was a spillover effect of this chivalrous sentiment, for he enjoyed a situation in which the dynastic struggles of his rulers did not regularly affect him.

One of the reasons for this respite was the emergence of positive international law as a substantive force in European politics. The numerous treaties entered into by the European states during this period have been exhaustively analyzed, and their recounting here is unnecessary. However, some of the newly formalized guarantees specifically pertained to the civilian. For example, the recognition of neutrality and neutral shipping rights, free passage of neutrals even between and into belligerent states, and the honoring of passports were all evidences of a general recognition that armed conflict should affect only the armed who were in conflict. Even among this group, military hospitals were established and their immunity respected, and prisoner exchange became commonplace. Finally, and in some respects most important, "academic" international law achieved an even higher status of respect and application. From the standpoint of civilian immunity, the most important author of this age was Emmerich von Vattel (1714-1767).

The Swiss-born Vattel combined a liberal education with a diplomatic career; his principal work, *Le droit des gens,* was

published in 1758.[7] In this treatise he summarizes the thought of
centuries with an eye to present application. In discussing the object of war, he sounds almost medieval: "The purpose or lawful
object of every war . . . is to avenge or to prevent an injury."[8]
His discussion of just war encompasses the by now traditional
and accepted norms. What marked Vattel as distinctly contemporary was his statement on the noncombatant.

He admits that "Women, children, feeble old men, and the sick
are to be counted among the enemy," and that as such, because
they belong to the enemy nation, a belligerent has rights over
them.

> But these are enemies who offer no resistance, and consequently
> the belligerent has no right to maltreat or otherwise offer violence
> to them, much less to put them to death. There is to-day no Na-
> tion in any degree civilized which does not observe this rule of
> justice and humanity.[9]

If violations of this immunity should occur, Vattel says, officers
should punish those of their men who are guilty of such breaches.
The same rule of immunity extends to "ministers of public wor-
ship and to men of letters and other persons whose manner of
life is wholly apart from the profession of arms."[10] Even
"husbandmen" and their property are immune from attack. These
protections for all categories are subject to only one qualification: Immune persons must not take any active part in the
hostilities; if they do, their immune status is forfeit. Vattel is unequivocal that a person is immune not because of sex, age, or
occupation, but rather because persons of certain categories normally do not resist or fight. To the extent to which this posture
is maintained, they must be guarded from any harm.

Two points in Vattel's arguments bear special note. The first
is that his frame of reference is the "Nation" as the basic element
of contest in warfare. A citizen, any citizen, of an enemy nation
is formally to be counted among the enemy. But though sovereign
nations may be at war, rights and responsibilities between them
are still in force and persons who are not actively fighting are,
even as enemies, entitled to protection as noncombatants. There
is in Vattel no hint of moral rightness or wrongness derived from

theological or philosophical sources. His advocacy is based on simple fact: Is the enemy subject fighting or not? If not, no harm will come to him. This leads to the second point.

Vattel's position is not as it was even for Grotius, namely, that noncombatants ought to be spared; rather Vattel says that they are and will be spared. This in itself suggests that the status of the civilian had by this time been confirmed not only as a theoretical ideal but also as an actual practice.

> At the present day war is carried on by regular armies; the people, the peasantry, the towns-folk, take no part in it, and as a rule have nothing to fear from the sword of the enemy . . . . They live in safety as if they were on friendly terms with the enemy; their property rights are even held sacred; the peasants go freely into the enemy camp to sell their provisions, and they are protected as far as possible from the calamities of war.[11]

Vattel was a recorder of his time. Yet his time was beginning to change, and not for the better for the civilian. Though another century was to pass before the civilian's status would be drastically altered, the elements that accounted for his relative immunity were shifting. The ballet interlude of military maneuver would soon succumb to the massed forces of people's armies facing each other in the Napoleonic wars. Reliance on mercenaries would be replaced by a call to nations in arms. Technological advances produced more and more efficient weapons. An ideological fervor, absent for a century, would engulf Europe in a massive struggle, resulting in a new European power alignment that would temporarily restore the civilian to his eighteenth century status but that ultimately would seriously challenge the permanence of that status.

The American Revolution was the harbinger of these changes. Edmund Burke, the Whig friend of the American colonists, defended it as a "conservative" revolution, in that the colonists were demanding no more than they deserved as English citizens. Indeed, this was perhaps the core complaint of most colonists. What began as a call for "redress of grievances," however, ended as revolution and a final rupture with England.

The conduct of the American Revolution is instructive. Typical of eighteenth century warfare, regular and mercenary troops were employed by the British. The conduct of troops toward civilians was generally exemplary, bearing out Vattel's earlier statements. This conduct was especially remarkable since the colonists were not officially an "enemy," in international terms, but rather "rebels" or the equivalent of internal criminals. Their status in international law was very questionable and their treatment was uneven. On balance, however, prisoners, property, and privilege were treated according to the accepted rules of warfare. Civilians were generally protected and neutrality was usually respected.

But several disquieting features emerged from this conflict. The rebels had the uncouth habit of fighting their enemies from behind rocks, walls, and trees instead of facing them in formal battle line. The American forces often wore no distinctive uniforms or identifying insignia, which allowed them to fade easily into the civilian population and thus avoid injury or capture. Many of the colonists were better armed than the British soldiery, since the general-issue English "Brown Bess" smooth-bore musket could not match the accuracy or range of a Kentucky rifle.[12] "Irregular" citizen-soldiers, disinclined to adhere to the rules of formal eighteenth century battle, equipped with superior firearms, and supported by a civilian population that grew increasingly hostile toward occupying British and Hessian troops, proved finally capable of "redressing their grievances" against the armed forces of the global empire. The conclusion was separation of the American colonies from their former political allegiance: in effect, a successful civil war.[13]

A significant body of the revolutionaries was imbued with the Rationalist ideology of Thomas Jefferson and Tom Paine, and could respond with conviction to the notions of inalienable rights to life, liberty, and the pursuit of happiness. An intellectual adherence to natural law and its obligations had been firmly replaced by its obverse, natural right and its claims. The Age of Enlightenment was about to give birth to the Age of Ideology. As Christianity and the *pax Romana* were successors to the forces set in motion by Stoicism and Alexandrian conquest twenty centuries before, so, too, would the forces at work in the American Revolution and its aftermath, ideological and technological, influence the shape and scope of coming wars.

Having succeeded in their "civil war" against Britain, the newly independent American states occupied themselves with establishing their own internal order. They were removed by distance and inclination from the affairs of Europe, and their "revolution" was not for export, for, as Burke had said, it was a "conservative" revolution, fomented and executed by men of substance whose goal was independence from an oppressive regime, not the overthrow of their society.

The year in which the Americans were completing their new political structure, 1789, saw the French dismantling theirs. Edmund Burke later would excoriate the French experience for being the opposite of the American: a "radical" revolution. Ironically, verbally identical concepts such as liberty and equality signaled different results in the two different contexts. For the Americans, the terms referred to accustomed but withdrawn rights; to a French audience, they pointed to a new experience. Rousseau's "democracy," taken out of context from his *Du contrat social,* became a slogan tolling the destruction of the *ancien régime,* of the entire European political system that had for a century effectively made war relatively safe for the civilian. With the French Revolution came conscription, a return to the armed horde, the *levée en masse;* in the eyes of more than one commentator, a return to the total warfare of primitive times.[14]

One incident growing out of the Convention's call for 500,000 conscripts is indicative of the ephemeral and delicate nature of civilian immunity. When conscription was declared, revolt broke out in *La Vendée.* To General Westermann is ascribed the following account:

> I have crushed the children under the hoofs of the horses, massacred the women . . . who . . . will breed no more brigands. I have not a single prisoner with which to reproach myself. I have wiped out all . . . . The roads are strewn with corpses.[15]

So much for Vattel!

Civil wars, wars of "liberation," wars of religion, and revolutions have traditionally been bloodbaths for the civilian populations. Often this has been true because many from the civilian populations have been involved in the conflict.

Two elements present in the French Revolution mark it as the prototype of wars to come: a nation in arms; and a people imbued with an ideological fervor, a sense of righteousness and mission that automatically precluded mercy, and with little adherence to traditional legal or moral strictures. It is again ironic that in the name of the new secular religion of *liberté, equalité, et fraternité* the comment of General Westermann should echo a similar chord struck centuries before in the same region. In 1209 a crusade was launched in southern France against the Albigensian heretics. When the besieged town of Beziers was about to fall to the royal and papal forces, a commander inquired of the Papal Legate, Arnold Amalric, how the soldiers should distinguish between heretic and orthodox believers. Amalric responded, "Kill them all! God will know his own!"[16]

The self-confidence of ideology has remained constant since man became ideologic. The French Revolution reintroduced to modern warfare an armed population imbued with an ideal. All that was needed to finally break the fragile peace between civilian and soldier, a peace tortuously developed over many centuries, was a new weapons technology. When the breakthrough came, the three major components of modern warfare conjoined to make the concept of the civilian obsolete: a nation armed, convinced of the justice of its cause, and equipped with weapons that could destroy its enemy anonymously and indiscriminately.

What is deceptive in the nineteenth century, so far as civilian immunity is concerned, is that the practice of warfare was not markedly different from the previous century. Once the Napoleonic tide had ebbed, the Congress of Vienna restored a balance of power. European and American wars (for example, Crimean, Franco-Prussian, Mexican) were fought for dynastic as well as political reasons. The political ends were limited, and the means employed were generally commensurate with limited goals. Enemies were definable and their soldiery distinguishable.

Wars of attrition against civilian populations were neither warranted nor permitted. The Clausewitzian dictum that war was a continuation of state policy was followed. Though a new weapons technology was evolving, its effect was felt by soldiers in the field, not by families at home.[17]

One conflict during this period stands out as a predictable exception to this pattern: the American Civil War, predictably different precisely because it was that most uncontrollable of human conflicts, a war within the polity. Conscription, ideology, and technology conjoined to kill more Americans than have died in all of America's foreign wars combined. But it was not only the citizen-soldier on both sides who perished. The civil population suffered as never before or after in American history. This point is easily seen from the comment of General William Tecumseh Sherman:

> We are not only fighting hostile Armies, but a hostile people, and must make old and young, rich and poor, feel the hard hand of war . . . . The truth is the whole army is burning with an insatiable desire to wreak vengeance upon South Carolina. I almost tremble for her fate.[18]

Since the history of civilian immunity is fraught with irony and contradiction, it is perhaps fitting that in this first of modern wars (albeit a civil war), while large portions of the civil population were subjected to its dangers, the first military code was published, which governed the conduct of armies in the field toward populations.

Francis Lieber, who drafted the code for the Union army, was a German immigrant to the United States who became a professor of history and law at Columbia College in 1857.[19] A friend of General H. W. Halleck, himself a student of international law, Lieber was commissioned in 1862 to draw up a manual designed to make explicit the rules of warfare for the treatment of prisoners and civilians. The so-called Lieber Code was signed by President Lincoln and in 1863 was issued as *General Orders, Number 100, Instructions for the Government of Armies of the United States in the Field.* Its originality of inception, attested to by all later authorities,[20] was indicated by Lieber himself in a letter to General Halleck:

> I have earnestly endeavored to treat of these grave topics conscientiously and comprehensively; and you, well-read in the literature of this branch of international law, know that nothing of the kind exists in any language. I had no guide, no groundwork, no text-book.[21]

General Orders, Number 100, as Halleck had predicted, was to have far-reaching influence outside the United States. It was adopted by the Prussian government for application to its armies in the Franco-Prussian war and served as the basis for similar English and French manuals adopted shortly thereafter. At the Brussels Conference of 1874 the Russian delegate credited it as the basis for the Conference.[22] Its ultimate impact was to be felt in the work of the later Hague Conventions.

When Lieber's Code is referred to as "original" it is not chiefly because he adds new substance to the materials of his predecessors on the subject of civilian immunity. Rather, he culled from vast sources and produced a coherent and concise handbook that could be easily understood and applied by commanders in the field. This was the real innovation of his Code.[23] The next step in affording the civilian immune status in both theory and practice was an international congress that would codify and ratify the rules of "civilized warfare" and pledge its members to abide by the norms and categories of noncombatancy. This occurred at the Hague in 1899.

The Hague Convention of 1899 and its successor in the same place in 1907 were correctly hailed by statesmen as precendent-shattering achievements. For the first time in history the world's major powers convened to discuss and agree upon norms of international warfare. Other congresses had been held previously, most notably in Brussels and Geneva, but none with such ambitious purpose nor with such lasting effect on the establishment of codified international law.[24]

The first Hague Convention was held on Czar Nicholas's initiative, the second at the urging of the United States. The topics covered at the two Conventions included all aspects of international law and behavior, from maritime law, to declaration of war, to neutrals' rights, to that of concern to us here—the status and rights of noncombatants.

There is no need to detail these dicta. It suffices to point out that, as of the first decade of the twentieth century, the policy commitment of the world's great powers included an amelioration of suffering in war on the part of innocent bystanders. These were now recognized in categories: as prisoners, civilian inhabitants of occupied territory, neutrals (specifically defined), hospital personnel. The rights of property, of religious practice, and of immunity from being taken hostage were clearly spelled out, as was freedom of transit and correspondence for civilians in occupied areas. The persons and property of civilians were not to be violated.

The first, seemingly peaceful decade of the twentieth century appeared to justify the Panglossian cant with regard to the civilian. Two centuries of relative respect for his position had culminated in formalized policy statements, further credentialed in positive international law, that future conflict would not make him deliberately or carelessly a victim of attack or despoliation. From the women and children clubbed to death in a cave in man's distant prehistory, to a Saracen harem ravaged by Christian knights in "God's name," through the merchants and pilgrims of the later-middle period of Western civilization, whose goods were seized and persons violated, to Sherman's march to the sea, the civilian had finally emerged as an object of respect, to whom a formal law applied and obligation referred. Augustinian "innocence," Thomistic "intent," medieval popular revulsion, Vitorian sensitivity, and Grotian rationalism had combined as theory with the practice and goals of nations and governments to create a synthesis of humane definition and purpose. But then something went wrong.

X

The Living Victim:
A Conclusion

The first ground handful of nitre, sulphur and charcoal drove
monk Schwartz's pestle through the ceiling: what will the last do?

Thomas Carlyle, *Essays*

History too often verifies man's antipathy for his fellowman; but
only in this century have writers come to use the terms "world"
and "total" when describing warfare. Two world wars and the
dread of a third have inured the mentality of many to the irra-
tionality of modern conflict. The fact that wars are not caused
by nor do they erupt from a spontaneous combustion of weapons
seems to be obscured. Wars are planned and executed by human
beings, and they lead to acts that are beyond recall. Wars become
the negation of politics, and their ultimate menace now makes
man an endangered species. There is grim and tragic irony in the
fact that some humans should be concerned today with the preservation of the leopard and the snail-darter fish, while all creatures
are under the threat of nuclear extinction. It is as though man's
most formidable weapon, his big brain, has been numbed into
impotence. The faculty that has enabled him to invade space and
to create weapons that threaten his world's existence seems incapable of confronting a stark reality: If major conflict should
again occur, it may be fought with nuclear weapons and escalate
to a level which will irrevocably damage life on this planet. Ignorance of or intellectual immunity to this fact is imbecilic folly.

The previous chapters have outlined the way in which the
human species slowly came to an intellectual awareness of its own
ultimate vulnerability. Wars might be fought for fun and profit,
but if, as an effect, women and children were constant casualties
of these fatal games, societies and ultimately the species would
be threatened. The idea gradually seemed to triumph that a species
cannot regularly massively eliminate the biological essentials of

117

continuance: a society or species that kills its females and their offspring in addition to as many young males as possible threatens its own existence. One result of this realization was civilian immunity. The concept annulled enslavement, turned the chivalric code on a new course, and finally established itself as a law worthy of respect, recognition, and legal sanction. Yet two world wars, perhaps an imminent third, and ruthless guerrilla conflicts portend that the civilian will soon fade rapidly into an unremembered past.

The complicated intrigues and alliances of Europe at the turn of the twentieth century culminated in a war no one really wanted but that few took steps to avoid. Strategy on both sides of the conflict was sterile, and tactics were quickly reduced to the artillery barrage and machine gun, the trench and barbed wire. Casualties were enormous and, in the West, in reverse ratio to the minuscule amount of land won or lost. But this war was markedly different from any of its predecessors in its sheer scope, and in the destructive capacity of the weapons available to the combatants. From Gallipoli to the outskirts of Paris and the English Channel, the machine gun, tank, railroad, dirigible, airplane, and poison gas involved more human beings in destruction in a shorter period of time than any previous conflict. Though civilians were not slaughtered, the distinction between soldier and civilian was threatened with assaults on nations by blockade, submarine warfare, and air raids. The modern era of the universal citizen-soldier had arrived, and no democrat or nondemocrat, soldier or civilian, would again be safe.[1] World War I ended with casualties counted in the millions, with a revolution in Russia that counted more millions of dead, with widespread hunger and malnutrition in Germany, and with a peace treaty as politically noxious as the German gas that caused over one-quarter of all casualties suffered by American troops in a year of combat.[2]

If World War I ushered in the era of the universal use of the civilian as a soldier, World War II extended this usage. In no country, on any side, was the civilian immune from compulsory service, as either a formal, uniformed participant or as an adjunct in the "war effort." Women making munitions in a factory and children filling sandbags for defense against air attacks were deemed enemies worthy of destruction.[3] In a sense, Vattel's criteria for immunity were adhered to: age, sex, or occupation does not automatically qualify one as exempt from military attack; "participation" in warmaking makes one a belligerent, and hence, a combatant. But as a combatant, according to Vattel, though subject to battle violence, one nevertheless retained the right to "quarter" or surrender, a right to one's property if rendered defenseless and harmless to the opposing enemy, a right to be respected as a person, even though a foe. What Vattel and his successors of good will could not have envisioned was a totally mobilized population armed with weapons of magnified power and reach that made no discrimination of age, sex, or occupation. Added were ideologies going infinitely beyond the old religious fanaticisms. Conscription, technology, and ideology combined to seemingly erase the concept and the reality of the civilian.

If Fuller is correct, that a weapon such as the musket eventually made the democrat, then the palm must be accorded to the airplane for destroying the civilian. Until the advent of the intercontinental ballistic missile, no weapon so changed the course of human warfare as did the airplane. Tanks and armored vehicles, introduced in World War I, were nothing more than sophisticated versions of Ján Žižka's "Wagonforts" of the fifteenth century.[4] But when man became capable of leaving the land, of transporting himself and tons of explosives hundreds of miles in hours rather than days, the strategy and tactics of warfare were altered. One nation was now capable of wreaking destruction over the whole of another nation. Strategy could include such things as destroying civilian morale along with eliminating urban transport, communications, and housing. Obliteration bombing of German cities was adopted by the United States and Great Britain in World War II. The German blitz of London was repaid in kind several times over in February 1945, when British and American bombers spent fourteen hours dropping incendiary bombs on the undefended and hitherto "open city" of Dresden. It is estimated that at least 135,000 persons perished in this raid near the end of the war, almost twice the number incinerated in the blast at Hiroshima.[5] The victims were mostly civilians; the city contained no targets of major military importance; Germany's imminent collapse was well known; air power's civilian destruction had been forcefully established. Then World War II ended, not with a whimper but with a very big bang.[6]

Since then have come the nationalist and radical revolutions of the "third world." Mankind now lives with two brute facts of conflict: the threat of nuclear war, and the reality of guerrilla or revolutionary war. In both instances the civilian, as traditionally understood, is obsolete, an anachronism subsumed under that modern triumvirate of conscription, technology, and ideology. To the extent to which nations are willing to assent to the apparent conclusion dictated by these three elements, our species deserves the fate of the dinosaur.

There is perhaps no more vexing fact in the latter half of the twentieth century than the reality of nuclear technology: vexing in that man's ability to harness the power of the sun can be used to create new energy to enhance his standard of living, and at the same time to create weapons that, if used, may eliminate all of the living along with their standards. The United States and the U.S.S.R., and an increasing number of other nations, have chosen to arm themselves with nuclear weapons. There are pressing political reasons for a nation to seek defensive strength with the most powerful available weapons. To prevent being bullied by another nation is a matter of vital concern; to defend territory against a powerful neighbor who would usurp an accustomed life and threaten traditional religious, political, and economic values are matters worth fighting for, as human history has amply demonstrated. Historic defenses of property, body, and values can be understood in political terms: man requires security from arbitrary attack and freedom to pursue a chosen mode of life, so long as it does not radically impinge on the lives of others. Man leads a "political" life, a life within a political community. He is an "ambivert," that is, a creature at once "one" and "of the many." He is a political animal, an animal engaged in politics, the resolution of his and other groups' conflicts. Politics ceases when war begins, for war and its attendant violence signals that compromise and accommodation are no longer thought possible. But war has usually been aimed at a political settlement.[7] Now it is time to inquire if any political or human end can be served by a major nuclear war.

Some years ago two philosophers, Sidney Hook and Bertrand Russell, engaged in a series of exchanges over their preference for being either "Red" or "dead." Hook argued that surrender to the Soviets would be a fate worse than death, while Russell maintained that, though a loss of freedom was certainly onerous, it was preferable to extinction, a condition in which a loss of freedom would hardly be noticed since no one would be alive to enjoy it. That such a confrontation between two eminent intellectuals should have taken place at all is indicative of a poverty of perspective. Both assumed the fact of nuclear warfare as a possibility, even a probability, and were trying to decide mankind's choices in the face of its threat. Russell was in favor of nuclear disarmament and was labeled a crypto-Communist by some of his critics. Pacifism is not popular, nor does realism enjoy much greater favor.

If the term "realism" has any substantive content at all it must include the notion of activity directed toward an attainable goal. Realistic pursuit of war aims, and preparedness for it, must be judged against this criterion. Neither Napoleon nor Hitler embarked on their extravagances with defeat in mind, later aberrations notwithstanding.[8]

A realistic approach, therefore, to modern nuclear warfare must contain a judgment on its relationship to political ends. After analysis of all the factors involved, the inescapable conclusion is that there are no political goals, that is, human ends or purposes, that could be promoted or attained by a large-scale nuclear war. No territory still worth inhabiting could be obtained; there would be few survivors to inhabit the worthless territory; and the values for which the war was fought in the first place would have disappeared as neatly as those who held them.[9]

British Major General J. F. C. Fuller was no romanticist of war, nor was he an idealist. The respected author of more than two dozen books on warfare, he was the acknowledged authority on tank tactics, earning himself the sobriquet "Tank Fuller." While his own country's general staff largely ignored his work, its counterpart in Germany did not; thus the blitzkreig. Fuller is the equivalent of a twentieth century Clausewitz. His ideas are worth considering as synoptic of many authors who have written on this subject. On the atomic blasts that ended World War II, he remarks:

> The very source of creative power had been tapped and transmitted into a catastrophic agent; the ultimate military expression of the Industrial Revolution had been reached, nuclear energy in the form of an explosive had led to the tactical grand climacteric in human conflict—it had eliminated physical warfare as a profitable instrument of policy. . . . [10] directly the political factor is introduced, in all wars except those of the most primitive kind, the destructive means employed to achieve a profitable end must be limited; for example, when in feudal times the aim of a king was to bring his truculent barons to heel, the primitive artillery of that period was found invaluable to deprive them of their power of resistance—their castles. But had its destructive effect been such that not only their castles, but their retainers, serfs, orchards and cattle within a radius of several miles would be obliterated, nothing would have been left to bring to heel—the means would have swallowed the end. [11]

He warns that "From the point of view of any sane political aim, all-out nuclear warfare is nonsense." [12] No sane person could argue otherwise.

But if it is true that sanity demands that nuclear warfare not occur, why do nations arm themselves at an increasingly rapid rate with weapons that, if used, would produce a wasteland, directly contrary to any human purpose? One answer to this question has been that the mere presence of nuclear weapons and the awesome finality of their use is sufficient guarantee that they never will be used; hence the argument that precisely because the consequences of nuclear war would be so awful, no rational or sane leaders could even contemplate resorting to it. Unfortunately this scenario overlooks that man's history has often been dictated by leaders, from Caligula to Hitler, who have been insane, irrational, or very stupid. Since the evidence of the species' record is of chronic predominance of war over peace, is one to assume that the past quarter century has witnessed a reversal in human nature, or at least in attitude, and that all of the world's present and future leaders have taken an oath of rationality? If this were so, why would the threat of catastrophe be required to keep the peace in the first place? A contention is made that the threat is what deters, which must mean that without the threat man would revert to his old ways of attempting to gain at the expense of his neighbors by force and violence. Apparently, from the internal logic of the argument, man has not recently assumed a more angelic nature. One need only recall how close the world came to nuclear war during the Cuban missile crisis in 1962, when preparations for such a war were actually made.

Proponents of nuclear energy, for both peaceful and defense purposes, are quick to point out that few nuclear accidents have occurred, nor have nations resorted to the use of nuclear weapons. Such a defense is only partly true. The Cuban missile crisis did occur, and the world was closer to a third world war than ever before or since. A breakdown in a reactor at Three Mile Island in Pennsylvania did occur in 1979, and raised new questions about the safety of these installations as a long-term power source. A computer malfunction at the North American Defense Command Headquarters (NORAD) in Colorado did occur in 1980, which incorrectly informed personnel that Soviet missiles were approaching the United States.[13] It is simply a *non sequitur* to contend that because something has not happened yet, it never will. But one may counter that if nuclear deterrence has worked, its potential danger of failure is worth the risk. Perhaps this is true, except that the stakes involved are so great and so terminal. Jet aircraft possess numerous backup systems, but they still crash; military defense systems have alternative procedures but still fail, often from human error. But where is the backup or alternative to a nonreclaimable misjudgment involving nuclear weapons? There is none.

If it is true that nuclear warfare is insane from a political point of view and that it nevertheless could occur because of technological or human failure, then the question posed before demands restatement: Why do nations arm themselves, at enormous expense, with weapons that they presumably never intend to use but that might or would be used through misjudgment or accident?

Most of man's history is a record not of rational calculation and plan but of accidental and unintended encounters with his fellowman and his environment. From wars and battles no one wanted to scientific discoveries no one foresaw, man has stumbled through his existence as a lucky survivor. Now with typical feckless abandon he finds himself in a situation that could make of him an unlucky victim of his own insouciance. That he feels helpless in the face of his own technology further belies the contention that a new age of reason has arrived. Nations have decided that their choice is not whether nuclear weapons should exist at all but rather under what circumstances they could or should be used. The "deterrence" theory concedes that if nuclear weapons are used, deterrence has failed, implicitly admitting, therefore, that nuclear war may indeed occur.

In one sense it is of course simplistic to refer to the "world's nations" in a decision-making sense, since it is unlikely that even half the world's population knows the word "nuclear," much less its implications for future wars. Leaders declare wars; citizens feel the effect. Even in the few functioning representative democracies, the ordinary citizen has little if anything to say about the weapons his government will or will not use in his name. The distinction between civilian and soldier is obliterated when nuclear warfare among modern nation states is considered. In a context so fraught with peril, it is appropriate to note another major irony: modern weapons technology exists in its destructive potential in inverse proportion to the number of citizens necessary to employ it. As warfare has increased in ferocity, the actual combatants (or manipulators of machines and computers, as distinct from those involved in their manufacture) has shrunk. In this sense, nearly everyone in nuclear war would be a noncombatant. In the most real sense, virtually the entire human race has become "the civilian." Any argument directed to his preservation is an argument against the general use of nuclear weapons and an argument in favor of species preservation. No other conclusion is possible.

Since insanity, vanity, and stupidity among leaders will no doubt continue in the future as in the past, and since nuclear war could occur by accident or choice, and since no poll of the human race has yet indicated that mankind has turned its back on self-preservation and opted for extinction, what ought the civilian to do? He has two clear-cut choices (in itself, a rarity in human experience). He can remain passive, or he can emulate Satan. We are told that God's favorite archangel, Lucifer, pronounced against his leader the words that sent him to hell: "Non serviam!" Perhaps today those words might be repeated by the civilian to his leaders—to avoid the same fate.

Since it is unrealistic to expect this to happen, what other option might be available? Given the historic and predictable competition among human societies for real or imagined goals, now exacerbated by ideologies that proclaim freedom or a new social consciousness, international cooperation seems less likely than ever. Yet though the human race has historically enjoyed fighting, there is no evidence that its members have enjoyed dying, even though some have relished killing. It is just possible that an age-old idea, born out of its time, has now found its time. The Stoic notion of *homonoia,* universal brotherhood, might now find its enforced practical counterpart in a world federation of dread.

Men are brothers as human beings, and there the familiarity ends. The disparity between the rich and the poor both within nations and among nations may not be greater than before, but it is better known and probably resented more. Ideological differences between societies and groups are no more rigid than in the past, but they are fortified by weapons never possessed before. These factors, among others, doom the Utopian dream of a federation of the world's nations, at least in theory. Realism presumably dictates a different course.

The concept of universal brotherhood may have to find its expression in a form different from the Stoic ideal, namely in a fraternity of peoples bound together not from mutual respect for each others' likenesses but from a fear of each others' lethal hatred and mistrust. Would it not be the final irony in the history of the civilian if human malevolence were to prove to be the glue to bind nations together in peace? But is this not precisely what deterrence theory proclaims, that a "federation of dread," which will never result in the use of nuclear armaments, already tacitly exists? Yet in 1981 more than half of the American population, according to random polls, expressed their belief that nuclear war with the Soviet Union was a probability in the forseeable future. At the same time, the President of the United States proposed the manufacture of new and more devastating weapons, ostensibly to close a "window of vulnerability" that supposedly existed vis-a-vis the arms superiority of the Soviet Union. And finally, this same leader expressed his belief publicly (albeit later retracted) that a limited nuclear war could be fought, and won, without inevitable escalation. It is obvious that deterrence theory and practice lacks credibility even with its most ardent exponents, while the constituency that the policy is aimed to protect is both confused by and pessimistic as to its value.

Though the civilian can no longer be distinguished as a separate category in nuclear warfare, he again becomes visible in guerrilla warfare. Many nations or emerging nations have become the stage for this type of conflict in the past four decades. Most familiar to Americans is the Viet Nam war, though in its history America has experienced this kind of conflict in its own Civil and Revolutionary wars.[14] Guerrilla war has gained much attention since World War II because of its increased incidence, but it is not new. Whenever citizens have risen in arms against what they considered an oppressive regime, or an occupying enemy force, they have generally been engaged in this form of warfare.

Contemporary studies focus almost entirely on this type of guerrilla activity, a citizen uprising seeking a political realignment by force. Whether called rebellion, insurrection, or civil war, the activity is labeled "revolutionary," in deference to its goal, and "guerrilla" as descriptive of its means, that is, the use of "unofficial" fighters—civilians—as the armed participants. This type of conflict is internal, a violent contention within a political community for political and ideological supremacy.

But the term guerrilla also applies to civilians in an occupied territory who carry on the war against their occupiers by means of sabotage, espionage, and other means. Many examples of this form of warfare can be cited from World War II, among them, Philippine and Chinese resistance to the Japanese, and Polish, French, Greek, Norwegian, Dutch, Russian, and Yugoslavian resistance to the Germans. The Japanese and Germans were especially brutal in dealing with this resistance.

Because the lines are so difficult to draw as to whether a conflict is an internal revolution (Castro versus Batista in Cuba in the 1950s), a rebellion, clearly criminal and without mass support (the "Weathermen" in America during the late 1960s), or a civil war, with one territorially contiguous political or ethnic group attempting to break away from a central authority (the Confederate States in the 1860s), the position of the civilian in these conflicts is nearly impossible to define. In these "internal" conflicts the rights of the civilian are ill-defined, even undefinable, precisely because his role is unclear. Is he manning the barricades against a legitimate authority and therefore subject to sanction as a criminal, or is the very question of legitimate authority itself the subject at issue, and has a moral and legal vacuum superseded existing civil law?[15] Many of the moral and legal questions of civilian status in this circumstance remain unconsidered and unresolved.

A much different picture emerges, however, when the situation is one of a civil population occupied by a foreign force. Here the rules of international law are clear and explicit. In Lieber's Code, the author made a very important distinction between "partisans" and what would today be called civilian "guerrillas." His distinction is worth quoting in full.

> 81. Partisans are soldiers armed and wearing the uniform of their army, but belonging to a corps which acts detached from the main body for the purpose of making inroads into the territory occupied

by the enemy. If captured they are entitled to all the privileges of the prisoner of war.

82. Men, or squads of men, who commit hostilities, whether by fighting, or inroads for destruction or plunder, or by raids of any kind, without commission, without being part and portion of the organized hostile army, and without sharing continuously in the war, but who do so with intermitting returns to their homes and avocations, or with the occasional assumption of the semblance of peaceful pursuits, divesting themselves of the character or appearance of soldiers—such men, or squads of men, are not public enemies, and therefore, if captured, are not entitled to the privileges of prisoners of war, but shall be treated summarily as highway robbers or pirates.[16]

Lieber, of course, was writing from a perspective not shared by those in the American South. For the Confederate States of America the aim was clear: secession, a severing of political ties with the former central authority and the reestablishment of separate, sovereign political units reminiscent of the status of the American states from independence to 1789 under the Articles of Confederation. The South's effort therefore was directed not toward siezing control of the government in Washington nor forcibly imposing its value system on the rest of the country. Rather it sought independence and recognition as a sovereign state, precisely what the original thirteen colonies successfully sought from Britain a century before. Lincoln steadfastly refused the Confederacy this status and instead maintained that the secessionist states were rebels and therefore not entitled to the rights and privileges of belligerent status. Rather they were still subject to the laws of the Union, and as such were internal criminals without international stature.[17]

Though Lieber shared Lincoln's view of the nature of the conflict, his distinction between partisan and guerrilla was to prove the basis for later thought on the status of civilian fighters against a clearly "external," opposing, and occupying force. Thus the Chetniks in World War II were obviously partisans: irregular soldiers, uniformed and clearly distinguishable as soldiers, continuing to oppose an invading German army in Yugoslavia. As such they deserved (but did not receive) the rights accorded regular enemy soldiery. Contemporary international legal opinion, drawing on the Hague Conventions and subsequent Geneva Conventions, cites four conditions that a partisan must meet in order to qualify him for protective status if captured: he must 1) be commanded by responsible officers, 2) have a fixed, distinctive sign recognizable at a distance, 3) carry arms openly, and 4) conduct operations in accordance with the laws and customs of war.[18] But herein lies the major contemporary problem not accounted for by the laws of war as presently formulated: that there are three varying situations in which the civilian may be involved or affected by guerrilla conflict but only one in which the present laws of war apply.

The first is the internal conflict of rebellion, insurrection, or civil war. Here, no international laws of civilian immunity apply, and it is doubtful that they will in the foreseeable future, so long as the sovereignty of the state system remains judge in its own cause.

The second situation, involving civilian or irregular troops—partisans by the above definition—describes a category of persons who if not obsolete are nearly so. Who but the most romantic today could picture partisan troops always carrying arms openly, displaying distinctive identification, recognizable at a distance (what distance, one might inquire?), and treating their hated occupying foe according to the rules of the Geneva Conventions? Even if these niceties were to be observed, it is doubtful that their enemy would observe them; as has been so evident in the past, a breach of fair play by one side soon escalates the level of cruelty on both sides. The day of the chivalrous Chetnik seems well behind us. Besides, the very advantage of stealth, surprise, and subterfuge, the most formidable weapons of the weaker guerrilla against his stronger opponent, would be forfeit, and with them any hope of victory. Yet this category of guerrilla warrior is the only one formally protected by the present rules of warfare.

The third category of guerrilla is the type whom Lieber described as engaging sporadically in raids and destruction, blending into the peaceful population when it served his purpose.

Such, he declared, should be treated like highway robbers or pirates.

The precise nature of the Viet Nam war will be argued ad infinitum. Was it a crass invasion by the North Vietnamese of their southern neighbors, supported by a "fifth column" in the form of the Viet Cong? Were the Viet Cong nationalist patriots seeking to oust an oppressive and undemocratic regime in the South in order to unify an artificially and illegally divided country? Was the government at Saigon a legitimate regime, defending itself against common criminals who deserved to be treated like Lieber's "highway robbers" or "pirates"? Was the United States merely supporting an independent ally on that ally's invitation, or was it propping up a corrupt puppet regime unwanted by the majority of native Vietnamese? Was the conflict a complex and confused result of all these facts and practices of all the parties involved? No answer will ever be given to everyone's satisfaction, nor is one offered here. Our immediate concern is the status of the true civilian.

Several facts about this war are indisputable. Civilians were killed in large numbers by all the contestants, both intentionally and "unintentionally," as the result of the application of the principle of "military necessity." The Viet Cong used every means of "cover" available; one of the most effective was the civilian population, which was alternately cajoled and intimidated into giving aid to the guerrillas. Following the Maoist dictum, the Viet Cong used the civil population as a "sea" within which they swam as "fish." They ruthlessly exploited civilians, though they also received voluntary aid from many whose sympathies were with them. They operated widely in rural areas as an ad hoc government. They were sometimes friend and sometimes foe to the civilian sea around them; but their presence polluted that sea for the genuine civilian, for it made of him a "legitimate" object of military attack.

The same rationale that was used to justify obliteration and area bombing by explosives and incendiaries in World War II, and that since has condoned the use of nuclear weapons against population centers, serves to justify the killing of civilians in this type of guerrilla warfare. It is true that U.S. Army official policy requires that care be taken not to harm civilians "unnecessarily," but "unnecessarily" is related to military necessity, the achievement of military victory, which is the highest priority. If victory can be obtained without hurting civilians, well and good; if this is not possible then unfortunately civilians will be killed. Given the priorities, no other conclusion is possible.

The issue, of course, is, Are the priorities appropriate? To this the retort must be, Appropriate to what? Unless military victory is viewed as an end in itself, it must be considered a means to a political goal, the restoration of peace and continued human activity. Guerrilla warfare is limited warfare and does not foreseeably compel the destruction of millions of people as does the prospect of nuclear war. Yet so long as the same juxtaposition of value priorities exists in its prosecution as obtains in preparation for nuclear war, so, too, is the civilian relegated to the role of an instrument in whose name war is planned and waged but one whose most vital interest, life, is forfeited in conflict. On the other hand, if only one side in a conflict respects the civilian, that side may find itself at consequent disadvantage.

The Viet Nam war was mankind's first televised war. Its danger and destruction were daily recorded and nightly reviewed in millions of homes throughout the world. Civilian suffering could be shared vicariously as never before. Details of the My Lai massacre stung many consciences and forced many more to enquire if the United States should be involved in a conflict in which such lapses could occur. The tragedy of My Lai and its counterparts, however, was that it and they could have been avoided.

How could such a slaughter of nonparticipating civilians be avoided when the "enemy" was virtually indistinguishable from the peaceful population? How, for example, could an American soldier be required to ask questions first and shoot later? The answer is that such a constraint could not be imposed under the existing circumstances. But it is precisely the "existing circumstances" that should be subjected to critique. The My Lai massacre occurred in part because American forces were nearly totally ignorant of what their own traditions and manuals had committed them to as the proper behavior toward civilians. That the armed forces of the country that introduced the first manual governing the actions of its armies in the field and toward non-combatants should be so remiss in instructing its officers and men one hundred years later can only raise doubt as to its military and political leaders' intelligence and sincerity. And the Nuremberg principles, detailing crimes against mankind in justifiable reaction to Nazi atrocities against civilians and prisoners in World War II, would seem to require closer attention by the nation that was their leading author.[19]

If the above seems hypercritical of the United States and its role in Viet Nam, it should not be so construed. In general the American soldier has acquitted himself with mercy and compassion far in excess of the soldiers of many other countries. Nevertheless, soldiers in the field will usually react according to their training and their commands. These in turn will reflect the attitudes and policies of their superiors. Dresden, Hiroshima, and Nagasaki would never have been bombed unless the orders had been given or approved by the highest authorities.

The political and military considerations that led to the decision to use the atomic bomb against Japan are still cases in the court of historical judgment. There may never be a verdict. What cannot be denied is that all participants in World War II were willing to sacrifice civilian life if it was deemed necessary to achieve military victory, and even—though some more than others—in the absence of any military necessity. Political policy since then has succumbed to the internal logic of weapons systems, as though these in themselves automatically dictate their use.

No solution to the complexity of guerrilla warfare at the cost of the civilian is of any avail if the contestants will not allow the neutrality or recognize the innocence of civilians. Such warfare is not new in human experience. But savage and cruel as he has often been, man, that formidable creature of nature that conquers nature, has had the power and the will to alleviate the suffering of his fellowman.

Policy decisions are made according to priorities, conscious or unconscious. The future of mankind, that is, the civilian, depends upon a choice among priorities. If man continues to choose life, with all its uncertainties, he must reject his present role of nuclear hostage. He must refuse to be used as a pawn in a megalomaniacal game of power in which terrorists proclaim that the end justifies the means. He must avow his ambivertance, his being at once an individual, with rights and hopes, and at the same time that he is a part of the main, one of his species who owes something to it because he is of it. He must finally affirm that his priority is life, and that he will settle for nothing else.

Notes

Chapter I

1. As recently as the 1977 edition of Webster's *New Collegiate Dictionary* the term's definition was prefaced by the italicized *archaic*.

2. A value is a norm or standard by which an individual or a group justifies its actions. Since values are of human origin (subjective in source) they are susceptible to abandonment or change. Since "absolute" by definition means immutable and limitless, no human value can be absolute. Though human values are not intrinsically absolute, they may become both objective and universal in the sense that if a number of people subscribe to a particular value, it is then an objective fact that they hold that value. If a value is held pervasively by man, e.g., self-preservation, it can be said to be a *universal* value. But since it can be voluntarily abrogated, it is never absolute.

3. Carl von Clausewitz, *On War,* p. 406.

Chapter II

1. The new field in biology—ethology, the study of animals in their natural habitat—has provided invaluable information on animal aggressivity. An examination of the now ample literature on this subject should begin with the work of Konrad Lorenz, one of the founders of the discipline, and his work *On Aggression.*

2. A debate has raged for more than a decade over whether man's violent proclivities are innate, as Lorenz, *ibid;* Anthony Storr, *Human Aggression;* and others contend; or learned, as most cultural anthropologists maintain. For the latter, see, e.g., Ashley Montague, ed., *Man and Aggression.*

3. The literature on this subject is also extensive. The modern classical reference in the field remains Maurice R. Davie, *The Evolution of War.* Cf. Quincy Wright, *A Study of War,* and Morton Fried et al., *War: The Anthropology of Armed Aggression.*

4. Davie, *Evolution of War,* p. 18.

5. *Ibid.,* chap. 3. Davie lists a number of exceptions in fact and legend, but stresses that, "with these few exceptions, war is man's business . . .;" p. 36.

6. *Ibid.*

7. *Ibid.,* p. 195.

8. Euripides *The Trojan Women* 740-98.

9. Sallust *Cataline,* ch. 1–10, frag. 11-12.

10. Hugo Grotius, *Concerning the Law of War and Peace in Three Books,* trans. Francis W. Kelsey, p. 734.

11. Plato *Republic* 469-71.

12. The word itself is derived from *civis,* a city dweller.

13. "He who is without a polis . . . is either a poor sort of being, or a being higher than man . . . (he) must therefore be either a beast or a god" (Aristotle, *Politics,* trans. Ernest Barker, pp. 5-6).

14. *Ibid.,* p. 3.

15. Cf. W. W. Tarn, *Alexander the Great,* p. 111. On Alexander's ideal of brotherhood, see Tarn's final assessment, pp. 146-48.

Chapter III

1. Tertullian *De idolotria* 19 (trans. in *The Ante-Nicene Fathers* 3:73) (hereafter cited as *ANF*). For the original texts referred to in this chapter, consult the standard compilation, J. P. Migne, *Patrologiae cursus completus: Series Graeca* and *Series Latina.*

2. Tertullian *De corona militis (ANF* 2:99).

3. See, e.g., Lactantius *De divinis institutionibus* 6.20 *(ANF* 3:187), and Origen *Contra celsum* 8.73 *(ANF* 4:668). For the many pre-Augustinian sources, Roland H. Bainton, *Christian Attitudes Toward War and Peace* provides an excellent introduction. For the relative position of these writers as authoritative spokesmen for the church at large see Igino Giordani, *The Social Message of the Early Church Fathers.*

4. The evidence indicates that up to 170 A.D. there was not a Christian soldier problem. Few were in the army, and most of these were already soldiers at the time of their conversion. By 180 A.D. however, many Christians were under arms, especially in the eastern provinces. Indeed, the famous *Legio XII fulminata,* the Thundering Legion, which served Marcus Aurelius in Armenia, was given credit for the providential rainfall that saved his army because its Christians had prayed to their God for victory. See Edward A. Ryan, S.J., "The Rejection of Military Service by the Early Christians," *Theological Studies* 13 (March 1952):1-32, and Adolf Harnack, *The Mission and Expansion of Christianity: The First Three Centuries;* also C. J. Cadoux, *The Early Christian Attitude to War.*

5. See R. W. Leage, *Roman Private Law.*

6. Augustine *The Problem of Free Choice* (trans. Pontifex).

7. *Ibid.,* 1.5.11-5.13.

8. *Ibid.,* 1.5.12.

9. Augustine *Letters* (trans. Parsons). This letter is no. 47, *To Publico.*

10. Augustine *The Problem of Free Choice* (trans. Pontifex) 1.4.1.

11. *To Publico.*

12. Augustine *City of God* (trans. Dods) 1.21. The accused perpetrators of the wartime atrocities at Nuremberg and at the My Lai court-martial, who maintained that they were merely following a superior's orders, could have cited Augustine in their defense.

13. For centuries Niccolo Machiavelli has been chastized as the author of the double standard in political ethics. In *The Prince* he clearly states that a ruler is permitted certain actions when he is acting as a public agent for the community's welfare that he could not morally or legally do as a private citizen. A close reading of Augustine reveals identical public-private double standards in the matter of taking human life, prompting the suggestion that the term "Machiavellian" be replaced by "Augustinian."

14. Augustine *Quaestiones in Heptateuchum* 6.10. Translations of most of the pertinent texts of Augustine may be found in John Eppstein, *The Catholic Tradition of the Law of Nations*. Valuable works on the Christian tradition of just war as it springs from Augustine include Yves de la Briere, *Le droit de juste guerre*, and Robert Regout, S.J., *La doctrine de la guerre juste de Saint Augustin a nos jours*.

15. Augustine *Quaestiones in Heptateuchum* 4.44.

16. Augustine *Letters* (trans. Parsons) (no. 138, *To Marcellinus*). Augustine repeats here what he had stated twelve years earlier in *Contra faustum*.

17. See the texts collected from various sources by Gustave Combes, *La doctrine politique de Saint Augustin*. Combes is an adequate guide to the sources but his citations are frequently inaccurate.

18. Augustine *City of God* (trans. Dods) 19.6.

19. Augustine *Letters* (trans. Parsons) (no. 220, *To Boniface*).

20. Augustine *City of God* (trans. Dods) 1.9. Cf. *idem.*, *Problem of Free Choice* (trans. Pontifex) 1.5.12.

21. For fuller discussion of this point see my article, "St. Augustine on War and Killing: The Problem of the Innocent"; also Bainton, *Christian Attitudes*, p. 92. For a differing interpretation see Paul Ramsey, *War and the Christian Conscience*.

22. See, e.g., Ambrose *De officiis* (trans. Eppstein) 1.27 ff.

Chapter IV

1. Marie R. Madden, *Political Theory and Law in Medieval Spain*, p. 19. This is a fine study for an assessment of the period; also Hans J. Wolff, *Roman Law, an Historical Introduction*; Ernest Brehaut, *An Encyclopedist of the Dark Ages: Isidore of Seville*.

2. St. Isidore of Seville, *Etymologies*, in J. P. Migne, ed., *Patrologiae cursus completus: Series Latina*, vol. 82 (hereafter cited as *PL*).

3. "Justum bellum est, quod ex praedicto geritur de rebus repetitis, aut propulsandorum hostium causa. Injustum bellum est, quod de furore, non de legitima ratione initur" (Migne, *PL* 82:639).

4. "Nam extra ulciscendi, aut propulsandorum hostium causam, bellum justum geri nullum potest" *(Ibid.)*. See Robert Regout, S.J., *La doctrine de la guerre juste de saint Augustin a nos jours*, p. 46.

5. Ives of Chartres *Decretum* 10.80 (Migne, *PL* 161: 718-27, 1316), and *Panormia* 7, 45 (Migne, *PL* 161).

6. For an account of Gratian's importance and a French translation of the portions of his *Decretum* that deal with war, see Alfred Vanderpol, *La doctrine scolastique du droit de guerre*, pt. 3, sec. 1. This portion of Vanderpol's work has been translated from the French with commentary by James William Somerville, *Gratianus in Jurisprudence*. Cf. R. W. Carlyle and A. J. Carlyle, *A History of Medieval Political Theory in the West*, vol. 2; T. Lincoln Bouscaren, S.J., and Adam C. Ellis, S.J., *Canon Law: A Text and Commentary*.

7. Vanderpol, *La doctrine scolastique*, pp. 67 ff. Cf. Yves de la Briere, *Le droit de juste guerre*, p. 28; *L'Eglise et le droit de guerre*, p. 77.

8. Cf. Regout, *La doctrine de la guerre*.

9. Alexander of Hales, *Summa theologica*, pp. 683-89. For an excellent

discussion of just war as punishment see D. Beaufort, *La guerre comme instrument de secours ou de punition,* esp. pp. 63-68.

10. St. Thomas Aquinas, *Summa theologica,* trans. Fathers of the English Dominican Province.

11. *Ibid.,* II-II, ques. 40, art. 1 (trans. Fathers of the English Dominican Province 9:501).

12. *Ibid.,* p. 502.

13. *Ibid.*

14. *Ibid.,* p. 503.

15. *Ibid.,* p. 502.

16. Cf. Regout, *La doctrine de la guerre,* pp. 84-85.

17. For an overview of the permeation of medieval thought by Roman law and on St. Thomas, see Paul Vinogradoff, *Roman Law in Medieval Europe,* and Jean-Marie Ambert, *Le droit romain dans l'oeuvre de Saint Thomas.* For the developing notion of nationhood, see Bede Jarrett, O.P., *Social Theories of the Middle Ages, 1200-1500.*

18. Jarrett, *Social Theories,* p. 185.

19. Aqu. *Summa* II-II, ques. 40, art. 1 (trans. Fathers 9:502).

20. *Ibid.*

21. Etienne Gilson has correctly summarized Thomas's views on private killing when he says, "The taking of life, one's own or another's, is in St. Thomas's eyes so serious an act that it can be said, in spite of apparent exceptions, there is *no case* in which this act is morally justified. We mean by that that in no case is it licit to kill with the intention of killing. It can happen that the pursuit of a quite different and legitimate end may necessarily involve us in killing. Even here the killing must not be willed for itself and as an end" (Etienne Gilson, *The Christian Philosophy of St. Thomas Aquinas,* pp. 313-14).

22. Aqu. *Summa* II-II, ques. 64, art. 7 (trans. Fathers 9:209-10).

23. *Ibid.,* art. 3 (trans. Fathers 9:200). Note here again the emphasis on "evildoers."

24. Joseph T. Mangan, S.J., "An Historical Analysis of the Principle of Double Effect," *Theological Studies* 10 (March 1949), p. 61.

25. *Ibid.,* p. 43.

26. Aqu. *Summa* II-II, ques. 64, art. 6 (trans. Fathers 9:206-07).

27. One of the most concise and authoritative discussions of the distinction between these two groups of jurists, plus their respective importance and influence for later thought, may be found in the introduction by Harold Dexter Hazeltine to Walter Ullmann's *The Medieval Idea of Law as Represented by Lucas de Penna,* pp. xv-xxxix. Ullmann quotes extensively from Lucas's *Commentaria in tres libros codicis,* ed. Lugduni (n.p., 1957).

28. "Hosti in bello capto miserendum est, dummodo futurum periculum non timeatur" (Ullmann, *Medieval Idea of Law,* p. 195).

29. *Ibid.*

30. "Quod universitas alicuius municipii debet, singuli de ipsa universitas non debent" (*ibid.,* p. 197). This view of Lucas's is at variance with that of Bartolus, who held that in a *civitas* all the members of the group were co-responsible for the actions of its ruler. Cf. Ullmann, *Medieval Idea of Law,* p. 195.

31. *Ibid.,* p. 197.

Chapter V

1. For an assessment of the military situation at the time, consult Fletcher Pratt, *The Battles That Changed History,* and Lynn Montross, *War Through the Ages.*

2. *Ibid.,* Montross, *War Through the Ages,* p. 98.

3. "The force which had won these victories [against the Vikings and Magyars] and saved Europe from a relapse into savagery and paganism of the north and east was that of the mail-clad horseman. What wonder then if his contemporaries and successors glorified him into the normal type of warriorhood, and believed that no other form of military efficiency was worth cultivating?" (C. W. C. Oman, *The Art of War in the Middle Ages,* p. 21).

4. Studies and interpretations of feudalism are legion. For a concise and well-balanced appraisal see Sidney Painter, *Feudalism and Liberty.*

5. The Roman Catholic Church owned approximately one-third of the land in Frankland at this time. Its administrators, unable themselves to use this land, hit on the device of the "benefice," in which an individual was given "title" for a time to a portion of land, often for life. Charles not only emulated the Church's technique but also expropriated its holdings for dispersal to his followers.

6. For an excellent examination see Ludwig Quidde, "Histoire de la paix publique en Allemagne au moyen age," *Recueil des Cours* (Paris: Librairie Hachette, 1930), vol. 28, sec. 3.

7. Painter, *Feudalism and Liberty,* p. 7.

8. *Ibid.* The lack of central political authority in France and the approximation to anarchy is one of the major reasons why the peace movement of the tenth century originated and flourished there.

9. Feudal institutions and a more or less developed feudal system existed in the major part of the Carolingian Empire; England after 1066; southern Italy and Sicily by 1000; the Crusader kingdom of Jerusalem after 1100; southern France, and Barcelona and Aragon in Spain; Bavaria, Swabia, and eventually Saxony by the thirteenth century.

10. Painter, *Feudalism and Liberty,* p. 7.

11. *Ibid.*

12. Quidde, "Histoire de la paix publique," p. 455.

13. Quidde points out that "l'idée de la paix est la base de tout le droit penal des Germains. Il existe donc le droit de se faire justice soi-même, et en cas d'homicide ce droit, selon l'opinion publique, devient plutot un devoir de vengeance sanguinaire. La faida, la guerre privée autorisée par le droit, s'étend sur toute la parente. Tandis qu'en cas d'infractions graves a la paix, il est defendu a la parente du criminel de lui donner son appui, celle-ci est engagée dans la (faida), s'il s'agit d'infractions ordinaires" (*ibid.,* p. 456).

14. Cf. chap. 32 of Charles's *Capitulare* of 802. The same prohibition appears in the decrees of 815. See Ernest Semichon, *La paix et la treve de Dieu,* 1:2.

15. It must be stressed that the peace movements of medieval Europe were wholly inspired by the desire to abolish this institution of private war.

16. Cf. Hoffman Nickerson, *Can We Limit War?*; Maurice R. Davie, *The Evolution of War;* Quincy Wright, *A Study of War;* and C. W. C. Oman, *A History of the Art of War in the Middle Ages.*

17. Oman, *History of the Art of War* 1:14.

18. *Ibid.*, p. 16.

19. *Ibid.*, pp. 56-57.

20. See J. F. C. Fuller, *A Military History of the Western World,* vol. 1, for a discussion of these and other points.

21. Montross, *War Through the Ages,* p. 102.

22. *Ibid.*

23. Quoted in Montross, *War Through the Ages,* p.158.

24. Nickerson, *op. cit.,* p. 64; see also Sidney Painter, *French Chivalry,* pp. 3 ff.

Chapter VI

1. In Germany the two movements are traditionally referred to as *Gottesfrieden,* though they were distinct for about one hundred years. See Ludwig Quidde, "Histoire de la paix publique en Allemagne au moyen age," *Recueil des Cours,* vol. 28.

2. Until the past century, historians believed that the Peace of God had its genesis as a formal instrument, a declared body of canons or pronouncements, about the year 1031. Peace movements were known to have existed for some time before this date, but it was generally supposed that no formal enunciation of rules had been made. In the middle of the past century Ernest Semichon published his definitive work on the Peace and Truce of God, dating the former's beginning in 988. Later research substantiates his claim. Ernest Semichon, *La paix et la treve de Dieu.* Scholarly studies of the Peace and Truce are rare and of limited value. The best and most recent work is by Dolorosa Kennelly, "The Peace and Truce of God: Fact or Fiction?" (Ph.D. diss., University of California, Berkeley, 1963).

3. The canons and decrees discussed here may be found in J. Mansi, ed., *Sacrorum conciliorum nova et amplissima collectio.* Decrees of the General Church Councils (though not those of local synods) may be found in M. F. Schroeder, trans., *Disciplinary Decrees of the General Councils.* Schroeder's commentary on the texts pertaining to the Peace and Truce are usually naïve and misleading.

4. Loren C. MacKinney, "The People and Public Opinion in the Eleventh Century Peace Movement," *Speculum* 5 (1930), p. 184.

5. No canons of this council are extant, but Mansi provides commentary. See Mansi, *Sacrorum conciliorum,* vol. 19, col. 103.

6. The peace movement spread to Catalonia by means of the peace councils of Narbonne, which the Catalonian bishops had attended. See Robert E. McNally, "The Peace Movement in Catalonia During the Eleventh Century" (master's thesis, Catholic University of America, 1953).

7. Mansi, *Sacrorum conciliorum,* vol. 19, cols. 483-84.

8. *Ibid.*, cols. 829-32.

9. *Ibid.*, col. 827.

10. *Ibid.*, cols. 912-14.

11. MacKinney, "People and Public Opinion," p. 204.

12. See Marie R. Madden, *Political Theory and Law in Medieval Spain,* pp. 58, 62.

13. Sidney Painter, *Feudalism and Liberty*, p. 91.

14. The story is told that King John of France, captured at Poitiers, was released from his English prison in exchange for a number of hostages. When one of the hostages escaped, the king voluntarily returned to prison. Similar accounts demonstrating the worth of a knight's word are related in Lord Berners, trans., *The Chronicles of Froissart* (New York: Collier, 1910), vol. 35.

15. Canon XIV, Second Lateran Council (trans. Schroeder, *Disciplinary Decrees*, p. 204).

16. Canon XXIX (trans. Schroeder).

17. It is true that among the Moslem jurists there was common agreement that noncombatants among the enemy should be left alone. Women, children, monks and hermits, the old, the blind and the insane were in this category. Some jurists also included peasants and merchants. These general rules were so qualified, however, that those taking part in a *jihad* (holy war), the Moslem equivalent of the Christian Crusade, could consider themselves excused from compliance with them. In the name of Allah or God, all acts could be justified when one was fighting an unbeliever. We should recall that the same great Council of Clermont in 1095, which gave papal sanction to the Peace of God, also called for a holy "Crusade of Christian men" against the infidel. The result, of course, was the First Crusade. For Moslem sources and commentary, consult Majid Khadduri, *War and Peace in the Law of Islam* (Baltimore: Johns Hopkins University Press, 1955).

18. The general lack of mercy Christians and Saracens showed to each other may be seen from an event that occurred during the great siege of Malta by the Ottoman Turks in 1565. Having finally captured Fort St. Elmo from the defending knights of St. John, the Turkish commander, Mustapha Pasha, ordered nine captured knights beheaded and their headless trunks crucified within sight of the other forts. When dawn displayed this sight to the defenders of Fort St. Angelo, the commander of the knightly order of St. John of Jerusalem, Jean Parisot de La Valette, ordered all Turkish prisoners beheaded. "While Mustapha's army was collecting the captured cannon in St. Elmo and making them ready for dispatch to Constantinople as trophies of war, they were disturbed by the boom of cannon. The large guns on the cavalier of Fort St. Angelo were firing at them. They were firing the heads of the Turkish prisoners" (Ernle Bradford, *The Great Siege*, p. 127).

Chapter VII

1. A good deal of scholarly folderol has resulted from the renewed interest in Vitoria, most notably that precipitated by James Brown Scott in *The Spanish Origin of International Law*. Scott argues that Vitoria, not Grotius, should be credited with the title "Father of International Law." The point is moot, yet Arthur Nussbaum in his second edition of *A Concise History of the Law of Nations* feels obliged to refute Scott and defend Grotius's claim. "Father" or not, Vitoria's originality can hardly be disputed. For an adequate exposition of the general political theory of the Spanish Late Scholastics, see Bernice Hamilton, *Political Thought in Sixteenth Century Spain*.

2. Vitoria *De jure belli* 15.430 (trans. John Pawley Bate in Scott, ed., *Spanish Origin of International Law*, Appendix B).

3. *Ibid.*, 18.431.

4. *Ibid.*, 18.420.

5. See, e.g., Honorio Muñoz, O.P., *Vitoria and War.*

6. "Le point capital sur lequel s'affirme la difference entre Vitoria et les auteurs du Moyen Age c'est l'idée, et son application effective dans le droit de guerre, qu'une violation du droit objectivement injuste et maintenue avec persistance *n'est pas necessairement coupable* " (Robert Regout, S.J., *La doctrine de la guerre juste de Saint Augustin a nos jours,* p. 183).

7. *Ibid.*, pp. 35-36.

8. Vitoria, *De bello,* ques. 40, art. i, no. 9 (trans. Gladys L. Williams in Scott, *Spanish Origin of International Law,* Appendix F). This work should not be confused with *De jure belli.*

9. *Ibid.*, no. 10.

10. *Ibid.*

11. *Ibid.*

12. *Ibid.*

13. *Ibid.*

14. Briefly, the Thomistic principle of double-effect maintained that an action from which an equally good and evil effect resulted simultaneously was permitted if only the good effect were intended or desired. John C. Ford, S.J., exposed the practical uselessness of this notion as an ethical criterion in his now classic, then prophetic essay, "The Morality of Obliteration Bombing," *Theological Studies* 5 (September 1944): 261-309.

15. "I reply that to slay them [obviously innocent persons] is not permissible, whatever military persons may say. The children of infidels may not be slain, *for they have not committed any injurious act*" (Vitoria, *De bello,* ques. 40, art. i, no. 10) (italics added).

16. Vitoria *De jure belli* 35.446.

17. *Ibid.*

18. *Ibid.*, 36.447.

19. *Ibid.*, 37.448.

20. *Ibid.*, 37.449.

21. *Ibid.*, 38.450.

22. Vitoria insisted upon this in two different contexts. His thorough examination of the various contingencies which may arise in war is a good example of Vitoria's concern to apply a principle to concrete circumstances in order to provide a practical rule of conduct.

23. Vitoria *De jure belli* 38.450.

24. *Ibid.*, 49.454.

25. *Ibid.*, 49.458.

26. *Ibid.*

27. *Ibid.*, 60.467.

28. *Ibid.*

29. *Ibid.*, 13.430 (italics added).

30. Bede Jarrett apparently misses the significance of the inclusion of these last two categories among those who should be presumed innocent in war. He points out that the classes mentioned by Vitoria are "the contention of Antonino which he himself had accepted from a previous age: it was part of the

primitive 'right of nations' the validity of which the early Church had taken from the Stoics, and which the scholastics—Aquinas, Scotus and the rest—so strongly defended." He concludes that when Vitoria "comes down to the details of the conduct of war, Vitoria is less original." Bede Jarrett, O.P., *Social Theories of the Middle Ages, 1200-1500,* pp. 209-10. Not only does Jarrett grossly oversimplify the extremely complex transformation that the Stoic concept of *jus gentium* underwent in its Christian translation, but he seems to confuse this concept in turn with the very different notion of "international law," which Vitoria himself was instrumental in formulating. See, on this question, Heinrich A. Rommen, *The State in Catholic Thought,* pp. 620-27; and Ernest Nys, *Introduction to De Indis et de jure belli relectiones,* pp. 89-90. Jarrett fails to perceive the greater precision of insight and detail with which Vitoria approaches the problem of the innocent in war.

31. Vitoria *De jure belli* 49.459.

32. *Ibid.* 42.454.

33. Cf. *ibid.*

34. Jose Manuel de Aquilar, O.P., "The Law of Nations and the Salamanca School of Theology," *Thomist* 9 (April 1946): 208-09. Cf. also Rommen, *State in Catholic Thought,* pp. 624-25.

35. Cf. Ernle Bradford, *The Great Siege.* Vitoria's influence on Bartolomé de Las Casas should be noted. The latter's reputation as a defender of the rights of the New World Indians under Spanish dominion is well known. Lewis Hanke's extensive publications on Las Casas have further enhanced his image; e.g., Hanke, *The Spanish Struggle for Justice in the Conquest of America.* In the famous debate at Valladolid in 1550 between Las Casas and Sepulveda, the former's defense of the Indians was based directly on Vitoria's arguments, developed thirty years before in his *De Indis et de jure belli relectiones.* This prolonged but abortive consideration long remained exceptional in its dramatic focus on the conquering West's relations with the then "Third World." Cf. George Sanderlin, ed. and trans., *Bartolomé de Las Casas: A Selection of His Writings*; also, Paul S. Lietz, "More's *Utopia* in America," *Catholic Lawyer* 2 (October 1956), pp. 340-49. Lietz points out that "In the *De Indis* and in the *De jure belli* he [Vitoria] laid down the principles concerning the moral and juridical personality of the Indian and fixed the legal status he was to have for almost the whole of the colonial period" (p. 341).

Chapter VIII

1. Francisco Suarez, *Selections from Three Works of Francisco Suarez, S.J.,* vol. 2.

2. *Ibid.,* sec. 7, p. 843.

3. *Ibid.,* p. 846.

4. John K. Ryan, *Modern War and Basic Ethics,* p. 35.

5. Suarez, *Selections,* vol. 2, sec. 7, p. 854.

6. *Ibid.*

7. *Ibid.,* p. 848.

8. *Ibid.*

9. That to the middle of the twentieth century positive international law was virtually devoid of a theoretical moral underpinning is amply demonstrated by the Nuremberg trials after World War II. Faced with an absence of specific prohibitions against genocide, the Allied prosecutors were forced to indict Nazi war criminals for "crimes against mankind," certainly a moral accusation and a laudable value judgment, but, due to its *ad hoc* inception, subject to the charge of imposing "victor's justice" on the war's losers. My contention is that if moral philosophy had continued to provide a critical theoretical basis for the positive law, no such hiatus in the law would have occurred.

10. Balthasar Ayala, *De jure et officiis bellicio et disciplina militari libri III,* vol. 2.

11. *Ibid.*, p. 45. Ayala was in error for, as we have seen, it was not always deemed disgraceful to harm women and children. His comment reveals his own acceptance of the prohibition.

12. *Ibid.*

13. *Ibid.*, p. 33.

14. Writing three decades before Grotius, Gentili devoted an entire chapter to arguing for the immunity of women and children in war, and another chapter urging the same for farmers, traders, and foreigners. "But we follow the laws of God which were made for all men, and the one of these which we are here concerned is, that we should spare women and children" (*De jure belli libri tres* 2:255).

15. Lynn Montross, *War Through the Ages,* pp. 285 ff.

16. *Ibid.*

17. Originally, Gustavus Adolphus imposed a strict code upon his troops. But as the Thirty Years' War wore on and Gustavus's army was diluted with foreign troops, discipline evaporated. See Montross, *War Through the Ages,* pp. 267 ff.

18. Hugo Grotius, *Concerning the Law of War and Peace in Three Books* (trans. Francis W. Kelsey), sec. 28, p. 20.

19. *Ibid.*, p. 722.

20. *Ibid.*, pp. 733-34.

21. *Ibid.*

22. *Ibid.*, p. 735. Grotius cites Vitoria as one of his authorities on this point.

23. *Ibid.*, p. 737. Again Grotius cites Vitoria, as well as Gratian's *Decretals.* The observation is worth quoting in full: "To priests and penitents you may properly add those who direct their energies to literary pursuits, which are honourable and useful to the human race."

24. *Ibid.*, p. 741.

25. Jean Jacques Rousseau, *The Social Contract,* p. 11.

26. Of these addenda to the binding law of nations, which Grotius himself refers to as *temperamenta,* Nussbaum has observed that they became the "most admired and successful parts of his work." Arthur Nussbaum, *A Concise History of the Law of Nations* (New York: Macmillan Co., 1947), p. 107.

27. For a recent general discussion of this point, see James Turner Johnson, *Ideology, Reason and the Limitation of War.*

Chapter IX

1. The importance of the Peace of Westphalia is universally acknowledged. Cf. Arthur Nussbaum, *A Concise History of the Law of Nations* (New York: Macmillan Co., 1947), pp. 85 ff, 293.

2. Jonathan Swift, *Gulliver's Travels*, pp. 267 ff.

3. Eymeric Crucé, *Le nouvlan cynée*, quoted in Roland Bainton, *Christian Attitudes Toward War and Peace*, p. 177.

4. See Bainton, *Christian Attitudes*, bibliography.

5. Quoted in Lynn Montross, *War Through the Ages*, pp. 379-80.

6. Bainton, *Christian Attitudes*, p. 185.

7. Emmerich von Vattel, *The Law of Nations*.

8. *Ibid.*, p. 244.

9. *Ibid.*, pp. 282-83.

10. *Ibid.*

11. *Ibid.*

12. Cf. Montross, *War Through the Ages*, pp. 417 ff. So important was the rifle in this conflict that Montross entitles his chapter on the American Revolution simply, "The American Rifle." Cf. John G. W. Dillin, *The Kentucky Rifle.*

13. The new nation would have a great impact on war by its armaments effort when Whitney innovated interchangeable rifle parts in the first decade of the nineteenth century. Montross comments accurately that "Thus Eli Whitney had made it possible to arm millions instead of thousands! With the exception of conscription—mass production of war's human material—no other factor has done so much to shape the fighting methods of the present day" (*War Through the Ages*, pp. 444-45).

14. The literature on this subject is extensive. For a comprehensive and balanced assessment of factors and forces at work, J. F. C. Fuller, *The Conduct of War, 1789-1961,* is excellent, especially chap. 2.

15. Hoffman Nickerson, *The Armed Horde, 1793-1939*, quoted in Fuller, *Conduct of War*, p. 31, n. 4.

16. See Barrows Dunham, *Heroes and Heretics*. According to tradition, the statement was: "Tuez-les tous! Dieu reconnaitra les siens!" I am indebted to J. William Hunt, Professor of Classics at the University of Notre Dame, for this citation.

17. During this period inventors and arms manufacturers were producing the breechloading rifle, rifled artillery, and the machine gun. Cf. Fuller, *Conduct of War*, chap. 5.

18. Quoted in Fuller, *Conduct of War*, p. 109.

19. Considering the impact of his work, it is curious that more has not been written on Lieber. Two introductory sources may be consulted: Bernard Edward Brown, *American Conservatives: The Political Thought of Francis Lieber and John W. Burgess*; and Elihu Root, "Francis Lieber," in *Addresses on International Subjects*. For the complete text of Lieber's code, see *The War of the Rebellion: A Compilation of the Official Records of the Union and Confederate Armies* (Washington, D.C.: Government Printing Office, 1899), series 3, vol. 3, pp. 148-64.

20. Cf., e.g., Root, *Addresses*, pp. 89 ff.

21. *Ibid.*, p. 91.

22. *Ibid.*, p. 93. For the regard in which Lieber and his Code were held, see the comments of his contemporaries in Root, *Addresses,* pp. 98 ff.; also Charles G. Fenwick, *International Law,* pp. 469 ff. Lieber makes the very imporant distinction between regular and irregular combatants, the latter called partisans. It is obvious that General W. T. Sherman, among others, was undeterred by the new General Order. This distinction will be considered in the following chapter.

23. See the section titles of *Lieber's Code,* indicative of the scope of his work.

24. For texts of these conventions, see James Brown Scott, ed., *Hague Conventions and Declarations of 1899 and 1907.* Cf. also Joseph H. Choate, *The Two Hague Conferences.*

Chapter X

1. For the effect on the civilian population in Germany of the Allied blockade, see J. F. C. Fuller, *The Conduct of War, 1789-1961,* chap. 10.

2. Fuller cites statistics indicating that 27.4 percent of American casualties resulted from gas. *Ibid.,* p. 174.

3. For an incisive analysis of twentieth century "force justification," see Robert E. Osgood and Robert W. Tucker, *Force, Order and Justice,* chap. 10.

4. Cf. Lynn Montross, *War Through the Ages,* pp. 187 ff.

5. For the raid on Dresden, see David Irving, *The Destruction of Dresden.*

6. Cf. Herbert Feis, *Japan Subdued*; and Len Giovannitti and Fred Freed, *The Decision to Drop the Bomb.*

7. Carl von Clausewitz has been quoted out of context perhaps as often as Jesus or Thomas Jefferson. He continually argues that war should never be viewed as anything other than a means to achieve a political end. For example, he says, "War is merely the continuation of policy by other means" and "war is only a branch of political activity . . . it is in no sense autonomous. . .;" rather "War is an instrument of policy." War, though it can be viewed as the antithesis of politics, if the latter is understood as the peaceful resolution of real or potential conflict, nevertheless remains subservient to political ends and purposes. (*On War,* ed. and trans. Michael Howard and Peter Paret.)

8. For one of the most recent and successful attempts to fathom the motives of Adolf Hitler, see Sebastian Haffner, *The Meaning of Hitler.*

9. The literature on limited and total nuclear war, both pro and con, is extensive. Some selected works are listed in the bibliography.

10. Fuller, *Conduct of War,* p. 303.

11. *Ibid.,* p. 313.

12. *Ibid.,* p. 314.

13. Apparently this breakdown occurred not once but three times, within a short span of time.

14. Once again, there is a large body of material on this subject, especially since the Vietnam war. Two works stand out as especially helpful introductions to the theory and modern practice of guerrilla warfare: Franklin M. Osanka, ed., *Modern Guerrilla Warfare*; and Sam C. Sarkesian, ed., *Revolutionary Guerrilla Warfare.*

15. See my article, "Urban Riots, Guerrilla Wars, and 'Just War' Ethics."

16. "General Orders, Number 100," in *The War of the Rebellion: A Compilation of the Official Records of the Union and Confederate Armies* (Washington, D. C.: Government Printing Office, 1899), series 3, vol. 3, p. 157.

17. Jefferson Davis, President of the Confederacy, unsuccessfully sought foreign recognition of the Confederacy as an independent state until the very end of the American Civil War. France and Great Britain were eager to grant it but not willing to risk U.S. antagonism.

18. All of the relevant documents are contained in two U.S. Army manuals: *The Law of Land Warfare,* Department of the Army Field Manual (FM 27-10), and *Treaties Governing Land Warfare,* Department of the Army Field Manual (Pam 27-1).

19. The record speaks for itself. Only after the unfavorable publicity from the My Lai incident did the United States' Armed Services take steps to formally instruct its combat soldiers on the requirement of civilian protection. The author became aware of this when he conducted a seminar for Pentagon officers on the morality of modern warfare. Prior to 1972, scant attention was paid to the rights of civilians under the Geneva Conventions. Subsequently, training films and lectures became a regular part of U.S. Army training, for both officers and enlisted persons. Lt. William Calley, the central figure in the My Lai affair, was both vilified and praised for his action. The reader should consult the relevant literature and draw his own conclusions. My view is that Calley and his immediate military superiors were guilty of violations under the Geneva Conventions, and that responsibility for their actions extended upward to the highest military and political levels. Cf. the trial and execution of General Tomayuki Yamashita after World War II in Taylor, below.

Two of the most influential books published on the conduct of American forces in Vietnam are Seymour M. Hersh, *My Lai 4,* and Telford Taylor, *Nuremberg and Vietnam: An American Tragedy.* See also Wilson Carey McWilliams, *Military Honor After My Lai.*

For an excellent assessment of the role of the professional military in Viet Nam by a soldier and scholar who was on duty there, see Sam C. Sarkesian, "Viet Nam and the Professional Military," *Orbis* 18 (Spring 1974): 252-65.

Bibliography

The following includes a complete list of sources cited and a select list of sources consulted. Those works with especially valuable bibliographies, introductions, or notes are marked with an asterisk (*).

Alexander of Hales. *Summa theologica.* Florence: Ex Typographia Collegie-S. Bonaventurae, 1924-1930.

Allers, Ulrich S., and O'Brien, William V., eds. *Christian Ethics and Nuclear Warfare.* Washington, D. C.: Institute for World Polity, 1961.

Ambert, Jean-Marie. *Le droit romain dans l'oeuvre de Saint Thomas.* Paris: Librairie Philosophique J. Vrin, 1955.

Antoninus, Saint. *Summa theologica.* Graz: Akademische Druck-u. Verlagsanstalt, 1959.

Aquinas, Saint Thomas. *Selected Political Writings.* Edited by A. P. D'Entreves. Oxford: Basil Blackwell, 1959.

——. *Summa theologica.* Translated by Fathers of the English Dominican Province. London: R. & T. Washbourne, 1917.

——. *Summa theologica cum commentaries Thomae de vio cardinalis Cajetani.* Padua, 1698.

Aristotle. *Politics.* Translated by Ernest Barker. Oxford: Clarendon Press, 1952.

Aron, Raymond. *On War.* Translated by T. Kilmartin. New York: Doubleday & Co., 1959.

Athenagoras. *Legatis pro Christianis.* In *the Ante-Nicene Fathers,* vol. 2. Grand Rapids: Wm. B. Eerdmans Publishing Co., 1951.

Augustine, Saint. *Contra Faustum.* In *Nicene and Post-Nicene Fathers,* edited by Philip Schaff. Grand Rapids: Wm. B. Eerdmans Publishing Co., 1956.

——. *City of God.* Translated by Marcus Dods. New York: Modern Library, 1950.

——. *The Problem of Free Choice.* Translated by Dom Mark Pontifex. Westminister, Md.: Newman Press, 1955.

——. *Letters.* In *The Fathers of the Church,* translated by Sister Wilfred Parsons, S.N.D., vols. 9-13. New York: Fathers of the Church, 1951.

——. *Quaestiones in Heptateuchum.* In *Patrologiae cursus completus: Series Latina,* edited by J. P. Migne, vol. 34. Paris, n.d.

Ayala, Balthasar. *De jure et officiis bellicio et disciplina militari libri III.* Vol. 2. Washington, D. C.: Carnegie Institution, 1912.

*Bainton, Roland H. *Christian Attitudes Toward War and Peace.* New York: Abingdon Press, 1960.

Baynes, Norman H. *The Political Ideas of St. Augustine's "De civitate Dei."* London: G. Bell and Sons, 1936.

Beaufort, D., O.F.M. *La guerre comme instrument de secours ou de punition.* The Hague: Nijhoff, 1933.

Beeler, John. *Warfare in Feudal Europe, 730-1200.* Ithaca: Cornell University Press, 1971.

Bennett, John C., ed. *Nuclear Weapons and the Conflict of Conscience.* New York: Charles Scribner's Sons, 1962.

Bethune-Baker, James F. *The Influence of Christianity on War.* Cambridge: Macmillan and Bowes, 1888.

Bittle, Celestine N., O.F.M. *Man and Morals.* Milwaukee: Bruce Publishing Co., 1950.

Bonet, Honoré. *The Tree of Battles.* Translated by G. W. Coopland. Liverpool: At the University Press, 1949.

Bouscaren, T. Lincoln, S.J., and Ellis, Adam C., S.J. *Canon Law: A Text and Commentary.* Milwaukee: Bruce Publishing Co., 1947.

Bradford, Ernle. *The Great Siege.* New York: Harcourt, Brace & World, 1962.

Breakthrough to Peace. New York: New Directions Publishing, 1962.

Brehaut, Ernest. *An Encyclopedist of the Dark Ages: Isidore of Seville.* New York: Columbia University Press, 1912.

Briere, Yves de la, S.J. *Le droit de juste guerre.* Paris: A. Pedone, 1938.

Brown, Bernard Edward. *American Conservatives: The Political Thought of Francis Lieber and John W. Burgess.* New York: Columbia University Press, 1951.

Burns, E. L. M. *Mega-murder.* New York: Pantheon Books, 1967.

Cadoux, C. J. *The Early Christian Attitude to War.* London: Headley Bros. Publishers, 1919.

Carlyle, R. W., and Carlyle, A. J. *A History of Medieval Political Theory in the West.* 6 vols. Edinburgh and London: W. Blackwood and Sons, 1903-1936.

*Center for Defense Information. *Defense Monitor.* Washington, D. C.: Center for Defense Information.

Choate, Joseph H. *The Two Hague Conferences.* New York: Kraus Reprint Co., 1969.

Cicognani, Amleto. *Canon Law.* 2d rev. ed. Westminister, Md.: Newman Bookshop, 1934.

Clausewitz, Carl von. *On War.* Edited and translated by Michael Howard and Peter Paret. Princeton: Princeton University Press, 1976.

———. *On War.* Edited by Anatol Rapoport. New York: Penguin Books, 1968.

Combes, Gustave. *La doctrine politique de Saint Augustin.* Paris: Librairie Plon, 1928.

Copleston, Fredrick, S.J. *A History of Philosophy.* vol. 2. Westminister, Md.: Newman Press, 1950.

Cronin, Michael. *The Science of Ethics.* Vol. 2. Dublin: Gill and Son, 1922.

Cunliffe, Marcus. *Soldiers and Civilians.* Boston: Little, Brown & Co., 1968.

Davie, Maurice R. *The Evolution of War.* Port Washington, N.Y.: Kennikat Press, 1968.

Diehl, Charles. *Byzantium: Greatness and Decline.* New Brunswick, N.J.: Rutgers University Press, 1957.

Dillin, John G. W. *The Kentucky Rifle.* York, Pa.: George Shumway, 1967.

Divale, William T. *Warfare in Primitive Societies, a Bibliography.* Santa Barbara, Calif.: ABC-Clio Press, 1973.

*Duffett, John, ed. *Against the Crime of Silence.* New York: Simon & Schuster, 1970.

Dumbauld, Edward. *The Life and Legal Writings of Hugo Grotius.* Norman, Okla.: University of Oklahoma Press, 1969.

Dunham, Barrows. *Heroes and Heretics.* New York: Alfred A. Knopf, 1964.

Eppstein, John. *The Catholic Tradition of the Law of Nations.* Washington, D. C.: Catholic Association for International Peace, 1935.

Falk, Richard A. *Law, Morality and War in the Contemporary World.* New York: Frederick A. Praeger, 1963.

*———; Kolko, Gabriel, and Lifton, Robert Jay, eds. *Crimes of War.* New York: Vintage Books, 1971.

Falls, Cyril. *The Art of War from the Age of Napoleon to the Present Day.* New York: Oxford University Press, 1961.

Feis, Herbert. *Japan Subdued.* Princeton: Princeton University Press, 1961.

Fenwick, Charles G. *International Law.* 2d ed. New York: Appleton-Century Co., 1934.

Figgis, John Neville. *The Political Aspects of St. Augustine's "City of God."* London: Longmans, Green, and Co., 1921.

*Fishel, Wesley R., ed. *Vietnam: Anatomy of a Conflict.* Itasca, Ill.: F. E. Peacock Publishers, 1968.

Flannery, Harry W., ed. *Pattern for Peace.* Westminister, Md.: Newman Press, 1962.

*Fried, Morton, et al. *War: The Anthropology of Armed Aggression.* New York: Natural History Press, 1968.

Froissart. *The Chronicles.* Translated by Lord Berners. New York: Collier & Son Co., 1910.

Fuller, J. F. C. *The Conduct of War, 1789-1961.* New Brunswick, N. J.: Rutgers University Press, 1961.

——. *A Military History of the Western World.* 3 vols. New York: Funk & Wagnalls Co., 1954.

——. *The Second World War, 1939-45.* New York: Meredith Press, 1968.

——. *War and Western Civilization, 1832-1932.* New York: Books for Libraries Press, 1969.

Ganghan, William Thomas. *Social Theories of Saint Antoninus from his "Summa Theologica."* Washington, D. C.: Catholic University of America Press, 1950.

Ganshof, F. L. *Feudalism.* New York: Harper & Row, 1963.

Generous, William T., Jr. *Swords and Scales.* Port Washington, N. Y.: Kennikat Press, 1973.

Gentili, Alberico. *De jure belli libri tres.* Vol. 2. Oxford: Clarendon Press, 1933.

Gilby, Thomas. *The Political Thought of Thomas Aquinas.* Chicago: University of Chicago Press, 1958.

*Gilson, Etienne. *The Christian Philosophy of Saint Augustine.* Translated by L. E. M. Lynch. New York: Random House, 1960.

*——. *The Christian Philosophy of Saint Thomas Aquinas.* Translated by L. K. Shook. New York: Random House, 1956.

Giordani, Igino. *The Social Message of the Early Church Fathers.* Paterson, N. J.: St. Anthony Guild Press, 1944.

Giovannitti, Len, and Freed, Fred. *The Decision to Drop the Bomb.* New York: Coward-McCann, 1965.

Gowans, Adam L. *Selections from Treitschke's "Lectures on Politics."* New York: Fredrick A. Stokes Co., n.d.

Gray, J. Glenn. *The Warriors: Reflections on Men in Battle.* New York: Harper & Row, 1970.

Greenspan, Morris. *The Modern Law of Land Warfare.* Berkeley and Los Angeles: University of California Press, 1959.

Grotius, Hugo. *De jure belli ac pacis libri tres.* Vol. 2. Oxford: Clarendon Press, 1925.

——. *Concerning the Law of War and Peace in Three Books.* Translated by Francis W. Kelsey. Oxford: Clarendon Press, 1925.

Guerdan, Rene. *Byzantium, Its Triumphs and Tragedy.* Translated by D. L. B. Hartley. London: Allen & Unwin, 1956.

Haffner, Sebastian. *The Meaning of Hitler.* Translated by Ewald Osers. New York: Macmillan Co., 1979.

Halle, Louis J. *Choice for Survival.* New York: Harper & Bros., 1958.

Hamilton, Bernice. *Political Thought in Sixteenth Century Spain.* Oxford: Clarendon Press, 1963.

Hanke, Lewis. *The Spanish Struggle for Justice in the Conquest of America.* Philadelphia: University of Pennsylvania Press, 1949.

Harnack, Adolf. *The Mission and Expansion of Christianity: The First Three Centuries.* Translated and edited by James Moffatt. 2 vols. New York: G. P. Putnam's Sons, 1908.

Hart, B. H. Liddell. *Why Don't We Learn from History.* New York: Hawthorn Books, 1971.

Hemleben, Sylvester John. *Plans for World Peace Through Six Centuries.* Chicago: University of Chicago Press, 1943.

Hersh, Seymour M. *My Lai 4.* New York: Vintage Books, 1970.

Hughes, Philip. *The Church in Crisis: A History of the General Councils 352-1870.* Garden City, N. Y.: Hanover House, 1960.

Irving, David. *The Destruction of Dresden.* New York: Ballantine Books, 1965.

Isidore of Seville, Saint. *Etymologies.* In *Patrologiae cursus completus: Series Latina,* edited by J. P. Migne, vol. 82. Paris, n.d.

Ives of Chartres, Saint. *Decretum.* In *Patrologiae cursus completus: Series Latina,* edited by J. P. Migne, vol. 161. Paris, n.d.

——. *Panormia.* In *Patrologiae cursus completus: Series Latina,* edited by J. P. Migne, vol. 161. Paris, n.d.

Jarrett, Bede, O.P. *Social Theories of the Middle Ages, 1200-1500.* Westminister, Md.: Newman Bookshop, 1942.

Johnson, James Turner, *Ideology, Reason and the Limitation of War: Religious and Secular Concepts, 1200-1740.* Princeton: Princeton University Press, 1975.

Kahn, Herman. *On Thermonuclear War.* Princeton: Princeton University Press, 1961.

Keegan, John. *The Face of Battle*. New York: Viking Press, 1976.

Keen, M. H. *The Laws of War in the Late Middle Ages*. London: Routledge & Kegan Paul, 1965.

*Knoll, Erwin, and McFadden, Judith Nies, eds. *War Crimes and the American Conscience*. New York: Holt, Rinehart, 1970.

Lactantius. *De divinis institutionibus*. In *The Ante-Nicene Fathers*, vol. 7. Grand Rapids: Wm. B. Eerdmans Publishing Co., 1951.

Lamb, Harold. *The Crusades*. Vol. 1. Garden City, N. Y.: Doubleday & Co., 1930.

Leage, R. W. *Roman Private Law*. 3d ed. London: Macmillan & Co., 1961.

Lee, R. W. *Hugo Grotius*. London: British Academy, 1930.

L'Eglise et le droit de guerre. Paris: Blond & Gay, 1920.

Levine, Robert A. *The Arms Debate*. Cambridge, Md.: University of Maryland Press, 1963.

Lieber, Francis. *Francis Lieber and the Law of War*. Edited by Richard Shelly Hartigan. Chicago: Precedent, forthcoming.

Lorenz, Konrad. *On Aggression*. New York: Bantam Books, 1963.

McIlwain, Charles Howard. *The Growth of Political Thought in the West*. New York: Macmillan Co., 1932.

McWilliams, Wilson Carey. *Military Honor After My Lai*. New York: Council on Religion and International Affairs, 1972.

Madden, Marie R. *Political Theory and Law in Medieval Spain*. New York: Fordham University Press, 1930.

Manncy, Albert. *Artillery Through the Ages*. Washington, D. C.: United States Government Printing Office, 1949.

Mansi, J., ed. *Sacrorum conciliorum nova et amplissima collectio*. Vols. 19–21. Venice, 1774.

Messner, J. *Social Ethics: Natural Law in the Modern World*. Translated by J. J. Doherty. St. Louis: B. Herder Book Co., 1949.

*Montague, Ashley, ed. *Man and Aggression*. New York: Oxford University Press, 1973.

*Montross, Lynn. *War Through the Ages*. New York: Harper & Bros., 1960.

Monument to Saint Augustine. New York: Dial Press, 1930.

Moore, John Bassett. *International Law and Some Current Illusions*. New York: Macmillan Co., 1924.

Moral Dilemma of Nuclear Weapons. Essays from *Worldview*. New York: Church Peace Union, 1961.

Morse, Arthur D. *While 6 Million Died.* New York: Ace Publishing, 1968.

Muñoz, Honorio, O.P. *Vitoria and War: A Study on the Second Reading on the Indians or on the Right of War, "De jure belli."* Manila: Santo Tomas University Press, 1937.

*Nagle, William J., ed. *Morality and Modern Warfare.* Baltimore: Helicon Press, 1960.

Nickerson, Hoffman. *Can We Limit War?* New York: Fredrick A. Stokes Co., 1934.

Nussbaum, Arthur. *A Concise History of the Law of Nations.* 2d ed. New York: Macmillan Co., 1958.

Oman, C. W. C. *A History of the Art of War in the Middle Ages.* 2 vols. London: Methuen & Co., 1924.

———. *The Art of War in the Middle Ages.* Ithaca: Cornell University Press, 1953.

O'Meara, John J. *Charter of Christendom: The Significance of the "City of God."* New York: Macmillan Co., 1961.

Oppenheim, L. *International Law, a Treatise.* Vol. 2. Edited by H. Lauterpacht. London: Longmans, Green and Co., 1951.

Origen. *Contra celsum.* In *The Ante-Nicene Fathers,* vol. 4. Grand Rapids: Wm. B. Eerdmans Publishing Co., 1951.

*Osanka, Franklin M., ed. *Modern Guerrilla Warfare.* New York: Free Press, 1962.

Osgood, Robert E., and Tucker, Robert W. *Force, Order and Justice.* Baltimore: Johns Hopkins University Press, 1967.

Pagès, Georges. *The Thirty Years' War, 1618-1648.* New York: Harper & Row, 1970.

Painter, Sidney. *Feudalism and Liberty.* Edited by Fred A. Cagel, Jr. Baltimore: Johns Hopkins University Press, 1961.

———. *French Chivalry.* Ithaca: Cornell University Press, 1957.

Peralta, Jaime. *Baltasar de Ayala y el derecho de la guerra.* Madrid, 1964.

"The Philosophy of War." *Monist* 57 (October 1973).

Portaliè, Eugène, S.J. *A Guide to the Thought of St. Augustine.* Translated by Ralph J. Bastian, S.J. Chicago: Henry Regnery Co., 1960.

Pratt, Fletcher. *The Battles That Changed History.* New York: Doubleday & Co., 1956.

Quasten, Johannes. *Patrology.* Vol. 3. Westminister, Md.: Newman Press, 1950.

Ramsey, Paul. *The Just War.* New York: Charles Scribner's Sons, 1968.

——. *War and the Christian Conscience*. Durham, N. C.: Duke University Press, 1961.

Regout, Robert. *La doctrine de la guerre juste de Saint Augustin a nos jours*. Paris: A. Pedone, 1935.

Remec, Peter Pavell. *The Position of the Individual in International Law According to Grotius and Vattel*. The Hague: Nijhoff, 1960.

Roland-Gosselin, Bernard. *La morale de Saint Augustine*. Paris: Marcel Riviere, 1925.

Rommen, Heinrich A. *The State in Catholic Thought*. St. Louis: B. Herder Book Co., 1945.

Root, Elihu. *Addresses on International Subjects*. New York: Books for Libraries Press, 1969.

Rousseau, Jean Jacques. *The Social Contract*. Edited by Charles Frankel. New York: Hafner Publishing Co., 1957.

Ruede, Ernest, O.F.M. *The Morality of War*. Rome, 1970.

Runciman, Steven. *A History of the Crusades*. Vol. 1. Cambridge: At the University Press, 1962.

Russell, Fredrick H. *The Just War in the Middle Ages*. London: Cambridge University Press, 1975.

Ryan, John K. *Modern War and Basic Ethics*. Milwaukee: Bruce Publishing Co., 1940.

Salisbury, John. *Policraticus*. Translated by John Dickinson. New York: Alfred A. Knopf, 1927.

Sanderlin, George, trans. and ed. *Bartolome de Las Casas: A Selection of His Writings*. New York: Alfred A. Knopf, 1971.

*Sarkesian, Sam C., ed. *Revolutionary Guerrilla Warfare*. Chicago: Precedent, 1975.

Schroeder, M. F., O.P., trans. and ed. *Disciplinary Decrees of the General Councils*. St. Louis: B. Herder Book Co., 1937.

Schwarzenberger, Georg. *A Manual of International Law*. 5th ed. New York: Praeger Publishers, 1967.

Scott, James Brown. *The Catholic Conception of International Law*. Washington, D. C.: Georgetown University Press, 1934.

——. *The Spanish Origin of International Law*. Oxford: Clarendon Press, 1934.

——, ed. *Hague Conventions and Declarations of 1899 and 1907*. New York: Oxford, 1915.

Semichon, Ernest. *La paix et la treve de Dieu.* 2 vols. Paris: Joseph Albanel, 1869.

Signatures, Ratifications, Adhesions, etc. to the Conventions and Declarations of the First and Second Hague Peace Conferences. Washington, D. C.: United States Government Printing Office, 1914.

Solages, Monseigneur de. *La theologie de la guerre juste.* Paris: Desclee de Brower, 1946.

Somerville, James William. *Gratianus in Jurisprudence.* Washington, D. C.: Law Reporter Printing Co., 1934.

Stone, Julius. *Legal Controls of International Conflict.* New York: Rinehart & Co., 1954.

Storr, Anthony. *Human Aggression.* New York: Atheneum Publishers, 1968.

Stratmann, Francis M., O.P. *War and Christianity Today.* Translated by John Doebele. Westminister, Md.: Newman Press, 1956.

*Stuart, Albert, and Luck, Edward C., eds. *On the Endings of Wars.* Port Washington, N. Y.: Kennikat Press, 1980.

Suarez, Francisco. *Selections from Three Works of Francisco Suarez, S.J.* Vol. 2. Oxford: Clarendon Press, 1944.

Swift, Jonathan. *Gulliver's Travels.* New York: Ronald Press, 1938.

Switalski, Bruno. *Neoplatonism and the Ethics of St. Augustine.* Chicago: Krol, 1946.

Tarn, W. W. *Alexander the Great.* Boston: Beacon Press, 1956.

Taylor, Lily Ross. *The Divinity of the Roman Emperor.* Middletown, Conn.: American Philosophical Association, 1931.

Taylor, Telford. *Nuremberg and Vietnam: An American Tragedy.* Chicago: Quadrangle Books, 1970.

Tertullian. *Apologeticum.* In *The Ante-Nicene Fathers,* vol. 3. Grand Rapids: Wm. B. Eerdmans Publishing Co., 1951.

——. *De corona militis.* In *The Ante-Nicene Fathers,* vol. 3. Grand Rapids: Wm. B. Eerdmans Publishing Co., 1951.

——. *De idolatria.* In *The Ante-Nicene Fathers,* vol. 19. Grand Rapids: Wm. B. Eerdmans Publishing Co., 1951.

Thayer, Charles W. *Guerrilla.* New York: Harper & Row, 1963.

Thompson, Charles S., ed. *Morals and Missiles.* London: James Clarke, 1961.

Tucker, Robert W. *Just War and Vatican Council II: A Critique.* New York: The Council on Religion and International Affairs, 1966.

——. *The Just War: A Study in Contemporary American Doctrine.* Baltimore: Johns Hopkins University Press, 1960.

Turner, Gordon B., ed. *A History of Military Affairs in Western Society Since the Eighteenth Century.* New York: Harcourt, Brace, 1953.

Ullmann, Walter. *The Medieval Idea of Law as Represented by Lucas de Penna.* London: Methuen & Co., 1946.

U.S. Department of the Army. *Law of Land Warfare.* Field Manual FM 27-10. Department of the Army, 1956.

——. *Treaties Governing Land Warfare.* Pamphlet 27-1. Department of the Army, 1956.

——. *Treatise on the Juridical Basis of the Distinction Between Lawful Combatant and Unprivileged Belligerent.* Charlottesville, Va.: The United States Judge Advocate General's School, 1959.

Vanderpol, Alfred. *La doctrine scolastique du droit de guerre.* Paris: A. Pedone, 1919.

Vattel, Emmerich von. *The Law of Nations.* Washington, D. C.: Carnegie Institution, 1916.

Vinogradoff, Paul. *Roman Law in Medieval Europe.* 3d ed. Oxford: Clarendon Press, 1961.

Vreeland, Hamilton. *Hugo Grotius, the Father of the Modern Science of International Law.* New York: Oxford University Press, 1917.

Vitoria, Franciscus de. *Commentarios a la secunda secundae de Santo Tomas.* Vol. 3. Salamanca, 1934.

——. *De Indis et de jure belli relectiones.* Edited by Ernest Nys. Washington, D. C.: Carnegie Institution, 1917.

Walker, James Bernard. *The "Chronicles" of Saint Antoninus.* Washington, D. C.: Catholic University Press, 1933.

*Walsh, Maurice N., ed. *War and the Human Race.* New York: Elsevier, 1968.

Waltz, Kenneth N. *Man, the State and War.* New York: Columbia University Press, 1959.

The War of the Rebellion: A Compilation of the Official Records of the Union and Confederate Armies. Washington, D. C.: Government Printing Office, 1899.

Wheaton, Henry. *Elements of International Law.* Oxford: Clarendon Press, 1936.

*Wiener, Philip P., and Fisher, John, eds. *Violence and Aggression in the History of Ideas.* New Brunswick: Rutgers University Press, 1974.

Wolff, Hans J. *Roman Law, an Historical Introduction.* Norman, Okla.: University of Oklahoma Press, 1951.

World Polity II: A Yearbook of Studies in International Law and Organiza-tion. Washington, D. C. and Utrecht: Spectrum Publishers, 1960.

Wright, Herbert Francis. *Francisci de Victoria: "De jure belli relectio."* Washington, D. C.: By the Author, 1916.

Wright, Quincy. *The Role of International Law in the Elimination of War.* New York: Oceana Publications, 1961.

——. *A Study of War.* 2 vols. 1942. Reprint. Chicago: University of Chicago Press, 1965.

Wright, R. F. *Medieval Internationalism.* London: Williams & Norgate, 1930.

Zampaglione, Gerardo. *The Idea of Peace in Antiquity.* Translated by R. Dunn. Notre Dame, Ind.: University of Notre Dame Press, 1973.

Articles

Aquilar, Jose Manuel de, O.P. "The Law of Nations and the Salamanca School of Theology." *Thomist* 9 (April 1946): 186-221.

Bourke, Vernon J. "The Political Philosophy of St. Augustine." *Proceedings of the American Catholic Philosophical Association* (1931): 49-50.

Brand, G. "The Development of the International Law of War." *Tulane Law Review* 25 (February 1951): 186-204.

"Crossbow." *Encyclopedia Britannica.* 14th ed.

Croust, Anton-Hermann. "The Philosophy of Law of St. Augustine." *Philosophical Review* 53 (March 1944): 195-202.

Delos, J. T., O.P. "The Dialectics of War and Peace." *Thomist* 13 (October 1950): 562-64.

——. "The Sociology of Modern War and the Theory of Just War." *Cross Currents* 8 (Summer 1958): 248-66.

Drury, George. "Theology of War?" *Cross Currents* 9 (Spring 1959): 192-94.

Ford, John C., S.J. "The Morality of Obliteration Bombing." *Theological Studies* 5 (September 1944): 261-309.

Garrett, Thomas M. "St. Augustine and the Nature of Society." *New Scholasticism* 30 (1956): 16-36.

Hartigan, Richard Shelly. "St. Augustine on War and Killing: The Problem of the Innocent." *Journal of the History of Ideas* 27, no. 2 (1966).

——. "Urban Riots, Guerrilla Wars, and 'Just War' Ethics." In *The Religious Situation,* edited by Donald R. Cutler. Boston: Beacon, 1968.

——. "War and Its Normative Justification: An Example and Some Reflections." *Review of Politics* 36 (1974): 492-503.

Hayes, Carlton. "Truce of God." *Encyclopaedia Britannica.* 14th ed.

Hula, Erich. "Punishment for War Crimes." *Social Research* 22 (March 1946): 1-23.

Johnson, James Turner. "Toward Reconstructing the *Jus ad bellum."* *Monist* 57 (October 1973): 461-88.

Kunz, Josef L. "The Chaotic Status of the Laws of War and the Urgent Necessity for their Revision." *American Journal of International Law* 45 (January 1951): 37-61.

——. "The Laws of War." *American Journal of International Law* 50 (April 1956): 313-37.

Lewy, Guenter. "Superior Orders, Nuclear Warfare and the Dictates of Conscience." *American Political Science Review* 55 (March 1961): 3-23.

Lietz, Paul S. "More's *Utopia* in America." *Catholic Lawyer* 2 (October 1956): 340-49.

McKenna, Joseph C., S.J. "Ethics and War: A Catholic View." *American Political Science Review* 54 (September 1960): 647-58.

MacKinney, Loren C. "The People and Public Opinion in the Eleventh Century Peace Movement." *Speculum* 5 (1930): 181-206.

McReavy, L. L. "The Debate on the Morality of Future War." *Clergy Review* 45 (February 1960): 77-87.

Mangan, Joseph T., S.J. "An Historical Analysis of the Principle of Double Effect." *Theological Studies* 10 (March 1949): 41-61.

Marin, Miguel A. "The Evolution and Present Status of the Laws of War." *Recueil des cours de l'academie de droit international de la Haye* 92 (1957): 629-754.

"Montanists." *Catholic Encyclopedia.*

Nurick, Lester. "The Distinction Between Combatant and Noncombatant in the Law of War." *American Journal of International Law* 39 (October 1945): 680-97.

O'Brien, William V. "Arms Control." *Social Order* 12 (March 1962): 131-36.

Quidde, Ludwig. "Histoire de la paix publique en Allemagne au moyen age." *Recueil des cours,* vol. 28. Paris: Librairie Hachette, 1930.

Ryan, Edward A., S.J."The Rejection of Military Service by the Early Christians." *Theological Studies* 13 (March 1952): 1-32.

Sarkesian, Sam C. "Viet Nam and the Professional Military." *Orbis* 18 (Spring 1974): 252-65.

Sibley, Mulford Q. "Conscience, Law, and the Obligation to Obey." *Monist* 54 (October 1970): 556-86.

Sturzo, Luigi. "The Influence of Social Facts on Ethical Conceptions." *Thought* 20 (March 1945): 97-116.

Unpublished Materials

Kennelly, Dolorosa."The Peace and Truce of God: Fact or Fiction." Ph.D. dissertation, University of California, Berkeley, 1963.

McNally, Robert E., S.H. "The Peace Movement in Catalonia During the Eleventh Century." Master's thesis, Catholic University of America, 1953.

O'Brien, William V. "The Moral Dilemma of Nuclear Weapons—Some Perspectives." Mimeographed. Washington, D. C., n.d.

Index